M000074256

Be a voice

4-Life

# ELI'S
## REACH

On the Value of Human Life and the Power of Prayer

# ELI'S
# REACH

## Chad Judice

**Acadian House**
PUBLISHING
Lafayette, Louisiana

ISBN 10: 0-925417-79-3
ISBN 13: 978-0-925417-79-4

◆ Published by Acadian House Publishing, Lafayette,
  Louisiana (Edited by Trent Angers; co-editor, Darlene
  Smith; produced by Bob Clements)

◆ Dust jacket design and production by Kevin Pontiff,
  Lafayette, Louisiana

◆ Printed by Sheridan Books, Chelsea, Michigan

*For all special-needs children
- God's angels among us -
and their parents*

# Acknowledgements

I would first like to thank God – the giver of all gifts and the source of all light and love – for His grace through the trying times we have faced as a family in Eli's short life.

I want to thank my wife, Ashley, for her patience, perseverance and willingness to sacrifice anything and everything for our children. Thanks also to my parents, Larry and Peggy Judice, and to Ashley's parents, Randy and Ann Guillotte, whose countless sacrifices on many weekends while Ashley was at work allowed me the time I needed to finish this project.

A special thanks is in order to my friend and spiritual director, Father Joe Breaux. I also owe a debt of gratitude to Trent Angers and the staff of Acadian House Publishing for their dedication to this project and their passion in helping to make it a reality.

I am grateful to all those individuals who contacted me after reading *Waiting for Eli* or after hearing my personal testimony and sharing with me how this story affected their lives in such positive ways. They continue to be an inspiration to me as both a speaker and an author.

I am very grateful to the families who allowed me to share their stories and faith journeys in this book. Without their cooperation this second book would not have been possible.

–C.J.

# Contents

# Preface

## *The continuing saga of Eli Judice*

I received a phone call from Chad Judice in the fall of 2010 saying that he was working on a new book, a sequel to his heartwarming volume titled *Waiting for Eli: A Father's Journey from Fear to Faith.*

I had edited and our company had published his first book, a thoroughly captivating story whose central character is Chad's son, Eli, a child born with a dreaded birth defect called *spina bifida.*

Chad explained that his second book would be about the impact of the first, about how Eli's story had motivated and inspired many who read it. In essence, it would be the continuation of the saga of Eli Judice.

At first, I was only mildly interested.

Then Chad pointed out that the new book would contain stories of two or three women who, after reading *Waiting for Eli*, had chosen to bring their unborn babies to term rather than abort them.

That got my attention.

I became more interested partly because I believe – that is, I know – that abortion is the taking of human life, an act that is rightly reserved for the Divine, not the doctor impersonating the Divine. Also, I was attracted to the project because every publisher worth his salt wants to publish "books that matter" or "books that make a difference."

A few months after that first call from Chad, I heard from him again. This time he told me he'd written a chapter about a guy who read Eli's story and, in essence, had a religious conversion because of it.

That really got my attention.

I could now imagine an intriguing bit of writing about how Eli's story touched the guy's heart and soul to the point that he was drawn away from a life centered on materialism to one that made a lot more time and space for God and family. It's a true conversion story that many of us would do well to emulate.

By now, I was starting to think that perhaps we should take a long, hard look at this manuscript.

But what sealed it for me was Chad's call to report a miracle involving his son that occurred on an Easter Sunday in a hospital in New Orleans.

Who wouldn't like to read about a miracle involving a precious special-needs child who survives a life-threatening medical episode?

How could a publisher say no to a book proposal containing such inspiring stories?

So, here we are again, now with a second book about a child whose story touches the hearts of readers, brings grown men to their knees, and evokes a keener appreciation of the value of all human life, including the lives of the most vulnerable among us.

*–Trent Angers, OFS*
Editor & Publisher

# ELI's
## REACH

# Chapter 1

## *That's my boy*

A few years before the birth of my second son, one of my students asked me to name my greatest fear. I paused to think for a moment then I told him it would be to have a child who was born with a mental or physical handicap.

My reasoning was that I didn't think I had the patience or the parenting skills to handle the added responsibilities that come with having a special-needs child.

As it turned out, I now have a child who was born with a birth defect. His name is Elijah Paul Judice. And he is one of the greatest blessings of my life.

He was born with *spina bifida*; as a result, he is paralyzed from the waist on down and wears braces on his legs. And he's the sweetest, most tender-heart-ed child you'd ever want to meet.

Eli is a beautiful little boy with rosy cheeks and a twinkle in his brown eyes, and he has caught the attention of people all over the United States. Actually, for being such a youngster, he's relatively famous.

His notoriety is due in part to the first book I wrote about him. It's titled *Waiting for Eli: A Father's Journey from Fear to Faith*. Now, I've written a second book, *Eli's Reach*, dealing with the impact of his story. I wrote this second book because I want to tell the world about the influence Eli's story has had not only on me and my immediate family but on the lives of others who haven't even met him.

Thousands read about Eli in my first book as well as in newspaper and magazine articles and online. Many of these same people have heard me tell his story in the talks I have given and continue to give around the country, from the Deep South to the Eastern Seaboard.

Just to put things in perspective, I want to explain that I am a high school civics and American history teacher at St. Thomas More in Lafayette, Louisiana; I've also served as a campus minister and basketball coach. My wife, Ashley, is a neonatal nurse at Women's & Children's Hospital in Lafayette. We are practicing Catholics and are of French-Acadian, or Cajun, descent. We were married in 2001 and we have an older son named Ephraim, born in 2005. Eli came into this world on February 17, 2009. We get a lot of help with the boys from our parents, Larry and Peggy Judice, and Randy and Ann Guillotte; they've helped immeasurably with childcare and in countless other ways.

Eli was diagnosed with *spina bifida* while still in his mother's womb. We never seriously considered abortion, though we had a very brief discussion about it – an emotionally charged exchange that lasted about a minute. The medical literature dealing with the detection of *spina bifida in utero* states that 80 percent of parents in the U.S. choose abortion after learning of this condition in their unborn children. Believing that abortion is the taking of human life, Ashley and I chose to bring our baby to term and to trust in God's providence. And we prayed long and hard for God's mercy, asking that He spare Eli the worst ravages of this dreaded birth defect.

When I write about Eli's reach, his influence, I'm thinking of his story's ability to soften hearts and change minds to a greater appreciation of the beauty and sacredness of all human life. Eli's story has influenced some to a stronger pro-life position and has even been influential in several pregnant women's decisions to reject abortion and bring their babies to term. I've observed firsthand how his story has awoken the dormant faith of some and drawn them back to sincere, heartfelt prayer.

Living with Eli has been an adventure. He's had more than his share of health problems, as all children with *spina bifida* do. He's had seizures and surgeries, emergency ambulance rides and hospital stays, with his immediate family at his bedside or in the waiting room or pacing the hallways, praying, always praying.

Ashley and I have seen things and been through things as Eli's parents that have scared the daylights out of us, even though we know that God is with us and with Eli. As we've traveled down the path of life with both of our boys – on our continuing journey from fear to faith – we have even witnessed a miracle, in a hospital in New Orleans on an Easter Sunday.

# Chapter 2

## *Sharing Eli's story*

In the months just after Eli's birth, I spoke at several small churches in towns around southern Louisiana, sharing Eli's story. I felt a calling to talk about the value of all human life and to relate how my wife and I were "walking by faith and not by sight" as we rejected abortion and chose life for our unborn son. I described how we had waited joyfully – and nervously – to welcome Eli into the world.

After one of the presentations, this one in the community of Port Barre, about 45 minutes northeast of Lafayette, I was approached by a young man with a somewhat anxious look on his face. A tall, handsome 16- or 17-year-old with a muscular build and wearing an LSU baseball hat, he walked up to me rather timidly and greeted me with a firm handshake. I could tell there was something he really wanted to say, something he needed to get off his chest.

"Mr. Chad, I had begun to doubt and really question my faith. But after hearing about your son Eli tonight, my questions are gone," he said with conviction in his voice, sounding very much like a guy whose faith had been rekindled.

Struck by what he said, I stood there speechless for a few moments. His words were so affirming. I realized at that moment the impact Eli's story was having on all types of people from all walks of life, from the very young to the elderly. I'd sensed it before, but I was dead-certain of it now: Eli's story has the power to change hearts and minds for the better, particularly on matters of faith and moral principles.

I also felt, more than ever before, that it was God's will for me that I should be making presentations such as this. This is exactly what I was supposed to be doing with my life: delivering this message about the dignity and sanctity of all human life, including the unborn, and witnessing to the power of prayer and faith in God's goodness and mercy.

In addition to speaking in churches and schools in various south Louisiana towns, I also gave a presentation – two, actually – at the Catholic school where I teach, St. Thomas More.

On the night of my first talk at STM, I was staring

out at maybe 300 people assembled in the mall area of our campus. Many faculty members were present, and I saw several familiar faces of parents and other individuals associated with the school community.

I spoke with passion that night, but I had the nagging feeling that many of the students who would have benefited most from hearing Eli's story were not there. I believed that for these students, hearing my testimony could help awaken their faith. Perhaps one of them who had never attended a retreat offered through our campus ministry program would decide to attend one. Or perhaps a student who was close-minded about the richness and spiritual benefits of Mass might make the effort to open his mind and heart and see something he had never seen or experienced before.

Among those who did attend was a student of mine named Chris Brewster. He's a popular guy with a broad smile and a great sense of humor – the type of student who brings life and energy to the classroom without being a distraction. He was there with his mom, Janet. The two of them were bright-eyed and seemed anxious to hear my presentation. Theirs are the kinds of faces every speaker is glad to see in the audience.

Another of the students who was in attendance that night is a girl named Adele. I saw her in our school's chapel a month or so later. She seemed to have something weighing heavily on her mind. She

# Area of Louisiana where Eli's story unfolds

wanted to talk.

"Can I ask you a question?" she inquired.

"Sure," I replied.

"When you and your wife were going through everything you faced with your son, how did you know God was there?"

I paused for a moment to think about my answer.

"I believed in what I had been taught my entire life regarding my faith. I had a choice to make: I could run away in anger or embrace everything I believe in. I realized that I was not in control, and the only person who could change the situation was God himself.

"I do not know what you're dealing with, or how bad it seems at this moment. But I can guarantee you that if you pray – and continue to have faith – something more beautiful than you can possibly imagine is going to come out of this."

She walked away seemingly satisfied with my answer but maybe not convinced.

A few weeks later, we happened upon one another again in the chapel. After prayer time, we resumed our conversation.

"Adele, do you remember the question you asked me last time we talked?"

"Yes."

"I have something to add to my answer. All my life I had been taught that God is love, but I didn't quite understand what that meant. During the moments when my fear had paralyzed me and I didn't believe I could pick myself up and keep going, I would look at Ashley and Ephraim. This inner voice kept getting louder and louder: *I love them too much to quit.* I was well aware of my own human capability to love. This love that was driving me was like nothing I had ever experienced before. It was the most powerful thing I had ever experienced. Love is not a feeling, it is a decision. That's when it all clicked; that's when everything I had learned before made sense. 'Whoever is without love does not know God, for God is love.' (1 John 4:8) That's how I knew He was there."

The warmth in Adele's smile said it all: She wasn't searching anymore; her eyes showed her newfound conviction.

Though it had been only eight months since Eli's birth, I could see plainly that his story, his life, was having an impact wherever it was known, including in my own school community.

\* \* \* \* \*

The week after my talk at St. Thomas More, our school community was shocked to learn that Chris Brewster had a brain tumor and had undergone emergency surgery. So, we began praying for his recovery and would continue to do so for several months.

A few days after the surgery, I received a message from Chris's mom, Janet, asking that I come over for a visit with Chris. She wanted Ashley and our boys to come as well.

I learned from a school counselor that Chris had been quite touched by my recent presentation of Eli's story and that his mom was moved by it as well. I understood from another source that ever since Chris was rolled out of surgery, his mom had been talking about Eli's story, apparently citing it as an example of a good outcome following a very delicate operation. She viewed Eli as a symbol of hope – hope that everything would be okay with her own son.

Ashley and I piled the boys into the car after school and drove to the Brewster home. I was nervous as I pulled into the driveway. I had never done anything like this before. I felt that the Lord was moving me way out of my comfort zone. Doing public ministry was already a stretch for a previously spiritually dormant guy like me, but to be ministering to someone in such a critical situation was a bit overwhelming. I prayed that God would use our family to give this family hope that all would be well.

Surprisingly, Chris answered the door. Besides the shaved head, and the semicircle of stitches resembling a horseshoe on one side of it, he looked like he could have been in class that day. Once I saw the smile on his face, all my jitters went away.

Janet hugged Ashley, then we all took a seat in the living room, with Eli sitting quietly in Ashley's lap. Ephraim played with some old toys from Chris's childhood on the living room floor. At first, Ashley and I mostly just sat back and listened as Janet talked, then the two of them started chatting about their common interests.

During the conversation Janet's eyes seemed to be fixed on Eli. After we had been there for 20 minutes or so, she asked Ashley if she could hold Eli. Ashley consented, then Janet stepped over and picked him up and sat down with him on her lap.

Once Eli settled down, he looked up at Janet and smiled. Their eyes met, and she smiled back. I could see tears of joy starting to form in her eyes. I think that seeing Eli healthy and thriving gave her hope for her own son, that he too would be okay.

And that's how it turned out. After having missed lots of school due to chemotherapy treatments, Chris was back in class four months after his surgery. Though he had lost his hair, he was still the same ol' Chris, laughing and joking around despite his brush with death. Everyone, especially the girls, seemed very excited to have him back.

After class, after all the other students were gone, Chris walked up to me and struck up a conversation.

"Coach, I wanted to tell you that after my last treatment, the doctors re-surveyed my body and said that they believe I am cancer-free," Chris said, smiling as he spoke.

I smiled back at Chris and told him I was sure it wasn't only the medical treatment but also prayers that got him through his crisis. He nodded at me several times and said he was sure of it as well.

# Chapter 3

# *The birth of a book*

My first book was born and released into the world in February of 2010, just a week before Eli's first birthday. Those were two good reasons to celebrate in short order.

Before the book came out, Eli's story had been told exclusively through my presentations at schools, churches and the like. The story was spread by word of mouth and via the social media. But that changed when the book was published.

Talk about a unique and satisfying experience! I can't compare it to any other experience I've had in life. *Waiting For Eli: A Father's Journey From Fear to Faith* was finally out in book form. Less than a year earlier, the book was just a hope and a dream. Oh, it was written and in rough manuscript form, but I didn't have a publisher and wasn't sure how to go about finding one. Of course, all that changed, and the book was edited and published in pretty short order, only six or seven months after being accepted for publication. I understand that's about one-third the time it normally takes from the signing of the author/publisher contract till the book sees the light of day.

Needless to say, I was on Cloud Nine for the book-release party. My whole family was there, as well as about 150 other people. A special prayer had been written and was read at the ceremony by Bishop Michael Jarrell, Bishop of the Diocese of Lafayette. The party was in a Diocese-owned facility. It was a night I'll never forget. My boys, Ephraim and Eli, were there, of course, and they were the life of the party.

Just a week later, Eli had his first birthday, on February 17. It was hard to believe that a year had gone by since his birth. (I know, every parent says things like this.)

One day I hope to be able to share with Eli the impact his life has had not only on our family, but on the lives of so many others. Our special gift from God continues to be Eli's presence in our home and in our lives. For others, it has been the impact his story has had on them individually and on their families.

This is clear to me from the letters I continue to receive saying Eli's story has strengthened their faith in God and their appreciation for the preciousness of human life. Lots of people expressed this to me, verbally and in writing, in the weeks and months following the release of the book. I heard from students, former students, colleagues, even complete strangers.

*Dear Coach,*

*Today around five in the afternoon I received your book. I read it in less than three hours. My parents would kill me if they knew I was up, but I feel I need to write to you. I am fighting back tears and have a face full of mascara right now.*

*I just want to say that without Eli and your family I probably would not be here. After I walked into your class for the first time in August, I went home and cried. Your passion and faith have helped me and others realize that without God we have nothing....*

*Tell Eli happy birthday and give him a hug for me. In his short year on this earth he has transformed many hearts.*

*- Anne Perret, Sophomore, St. Thomas More*

*Dear Coach Judice,*

*I graduated STM last year and have just started my second semester of college at LSU. I know we talked at school last year every once in a while and I was aware of your situation and prayed for Eli.*

*Today, my parents picked up my brother and me*

from Baton Rouge. We are heading to Colorado for Mardi Gras. When my mom picked me up, I learned that she had bought six copies of your book.

I started reading on the flight to Houston and finished on the flight to Colorado, where I am currently writing this e-mail. Your book and Wild at Heart by John Eldredge are the only two that I have really loved reading outside of school.

My mom gave one to my girlfriend, and right now it looks like she will finish it soon  because although the plane is shaking, she is still reading.

Thank you for sharing Eli's story....Your book has taught me that prayer does work and that I am making a difference when I pray. God is listening and He cares what I say.

Thank you,

S. Harrison Breaud

# Chapter 4

# 'Why me? Why my daughter?'

When Danielle Leger of Lafayette, La., gave birth to her daughter, Nadia, in the spring of 2009, she was filled with joy and optimism over the life that lay ahead for her and her baby.

Infatuated with the idea of being a mother and enjoying all the incredible experiences that brings, Danielle was slow to realize that something was not right with her daughter. She took Nadia to see an ophthalmologist, who observed a problem with the vision in the baby's right eye. An MRI revealed the optic nerve was underdeveloped. As a result, she would be blind in that eye for the rest of her life. And there was no guarantee Nadia would retain the vision in her other eye.

With this bad news, Danielle's dreams for her

daughter's happy, fulfilling life began fading away quickly. Tears rolled down her face as she drove home in what seemed like a tunnel of darkness. She was numb and hardly able to believe what she heard from the doctor.

*If she's blind, how will my child ever be self-sufficient and independent as an adult?* Danielle thought.

Anxious to become educated about Nadia's condition, Danielle sought the support of others. Numerous phone calls played themselves out like a broken record: "We don't have a support group for that condition, but we'll pray for you and your daughter." The more times she heard that response the more frustrated and depressed she became. She was thankful for the concern that was expressed, but it was not helping with the feeling of fear that was tearing away at her inside.

When Nadia was nine months old, she was diagnosed with another medical issue: uncontrollable movement of the eyes. She underwent a delicate surgical procedure to mitigate the problem.

Not long after the surgery, Danielle received more bad news. Doctors said Nadia appeared to be very small for her age – a condition that could be caused by a deficiency of growth hormone. Tests showed that indeed this was the problem. To correct it, daily injections would be required for an indefinite period.

Danielle's frustration continued to grow as she could only stand by and watch her daughter's sight deteriorate knowing there was nothing she could do to help.

*Why me, Lord?* she asked. *Why my daughter?*

Right before Christmas of 2011 Danielle received a definitive diagnosis from her daughter's endocrinologist. Nadia had a condition called septo-optic dysplasia. This typically causes blindness in one or both eyes while rendering the patients mentally delayed as well as giving them the appearance of being mentally disabled. To Danielle, this diagnosis translated to a lifetime of walking in the unknown. Her daughter could be plagued with seizures and delayed physical development. Hours of physical therapy and sacrifice lay ahead.

At this point Danielle was asking new questions: *Does anyone else really know how this feels? If they do, where are they?*

It turns out that, yes, there are others in the world who know what it feels like to have a child with a disability. And fate brought Danielle in contact with one such family – my family – in the spring of 2012.

She was at work, waitressing at Hub City Diner in Lafayette. At the table she was waiting on were my wife, Ashley; my boys, Ephraim and Eli; and my parents, Larry and Peggy Judice.

Danielle had waited on this group several times before. But this time she took special notice of Eli – the braces on his legs, the twinkle in his eye, his happy disposition. And he spoke to her – just chattering away about anything and everything. She was captivated by the little guy and noticed especially how happy he seemed to be despite his disability.

As they continued to chat, she felt a stronger and stronger connection to him, and a sense of peace. She even talked about taking him home with her to play with her daughter, Nadia, who was the same age as Eli.

At this point, Ashley mentioned to Danielle that I had written a book about my experiences as a parent of a child with special needs.

Danielle was so fascinated with Eli, and with the prospects of learning more about him, that when her shift was over she went out and bought the book.

Moved by Eli's story, Danielle wrote to me shortly after reading the book.

> *Chad,*
>
> *I am writing to let you know the tremendous impact* Waiting for Eli *has had on my life. My daughter Nadia was born April 16, 2009, and was diagnosed with a brain disorder in late 2011. My walk with her has been a painful and emotional journey.*
>
> *We have seen numerous specialists, been through endless testing, multiple MRI's, and a crucial surgery with the possibility of more in sight. I had no faith, and in my difficulty in accepting and dealing with these things, I turned away from God and always asked, Why me? Most of all I asked, Why my daughter?*

I tried calling several places searching for a support group for parents with a child whose condition was like Nadia's, with little or no success. They offered prayers, which at the time seemed nice, but never really seemed to be what I needed.

I bought your book today and I read it in one sitting. As I finished I couldn't help realizing – WOW! – I found my support group. The feeling I had cannot be described. It was as if God himself was speaking to me through Eli's story.

While reading I had flashbacks of the many random miracles that happened to us, but because I was so focused on the problems I missed out on embracing my beautiful daughter and her perfect imperfections. I am ready to embrace the "unknown" because Nadia is my unknown and I have been chosen by God for her and her for me.

She is the most amazing person I have ever met. Ironically, her name means "Hope" and that is something I will continue to hold on to for the rest of my life.

Eli's story has inspired me to rekindle my relationship with God and to begin attending Mass again. Your book has shown me that all this time instead of asking God why this was happening to me I should have been telling Him, "Thank you for choosing me."

I couldn't imagine my life being any different, and I don't want it to be. This story has opened my eyes, and Eli will forever be in my heart.

God bless you and your family,
Danielle Leger

# Chapter 5

# *A voice from prison*

Ashley and I have been gratified by the outpouring of love and concern for Eli. We've been deeply moved by many of the letters we received saying how Eli's story has touched the hearts and souls of those who've read about his life.

But nothing affected us more profoundly than a letter we received from an inmate at a correctional facility at Zachary, La., near Baton Rouge. It convinced us that our son's very existence – the story of his birth, his struggles, and our triumphs as a family – has the sublime power to melt hearts and bring people to a better understanding of the miracle and the beauty of all human life.

The letter came to us in August of 2010, just a few days before the start of a new school year at St.

Thomas More. It was in an envelope inside another envelope, relayed by two local prison ministers who had given a copy of *Waiting For Eli* to this inmate. He read the book and enjoyed it and asked them to see that Ashley and I got his letter.

Ashley sat on the sofa, and I read aloud as I paced the floor in our living room.

*Dear Mr. & Mrs. Judice:*

*My name is Dale Gaudet. I am a trustee at the State Police Barracks in Zachary, Louisiana. Before being transferred here three years ago, I was housed at Angola State Prison, where I worked for the Chaplains' Department and was a Catholic Eucharistic minister for 12 years.*

*I am sure that you have received numerous letters and e-mails from people whose lives were touched by your son's birth. Sharing your faith and vulnerability in this book has also touched my little community.*

*I loaned your book to one of the inmates here last week. He quit coming to church over 30 years ago and had basically given up on God when he came to prison. He is a loner, and although I have invited him to Mass time and time again, he has repeatedly refused my offer.*

*Then, last night, he returned the book to me with tears streaming down his face and asked me if I knew how your little boy was doing. I told him that I didn't know. But if he wanted we could pray for your family.*

It was the first time in 30 years he prayed the
Lord's Prayer.

Please know that your story has affected me as a
father and a grandfather, and I hope to share your
faith with my daughters on our next visit. I ask for
your prayers for me and my family. Please know that
I will continue to pray for Eli and your family in my
daily novenas to St. Jude.

God's Peace,
Dale Gaudet

Ashley and I were stunned by the letter, amazed at
its poignancy. So were my students when I shared it
with them. I often do a reading, a little spiritual reflection, prior to the prayers that begin each of my classes.
As I was reading the letter, I looked up and saw the
expressions on the faces of my students. I had their
complete attention.

That night, when I got home I sat down at my computer and wrote back to Dale.

Dale,

I wanted to respond to the powerful witness you
sent to me. I was so moved by what you wrote that I
decided to use it as a reflection in my classes today....

...The students were moved by the story you shared
regarding your fellow inmate who gave up on God for
over 30 years....

I asked them to reflect on Christ's words to his disciples, "If you have faith the size of a mustard seed you can move a mountain." Then I told them a man who had given up on God was moved by Eli's story to pray for the first time in 30 years....

Mountain moved!

Nothing else needed to be said. They got it.

Please let your friend know that Eli is doing better than ever expected, but that we are still in need of prayer. I request that you go to your fellow inmate and ask him to join you in prayer again on behalf of Eli. His willingness to pray after he read the book was his first acceptance of God's invitation to come home. If he is hesitant to pray, please tell him the father of the baby he asked about is requesting prayers.

May God continue to bless your ministry and may your witness continue to win hearts and minds for His kingdom!

Peace in Christ,
Chad Judice

I eagerly awaited Dale's response. I was anxious to know more about him and others like him who had been influenced by a story of a child they'd never met. A week or two after writing to him I went to my box in the teacher's lounge and found a hand-addressed envelope with my name on it. I pulled it out and smiled. It was from Dale Gaudet.

# Chapter 6

## *An inmate's burden*

I took Dale's letter to read during my prayer time in the chapel. Dale briefly thanked me for the update on Eli and said he had shared my letter with many other inmates when they gathered for monthly Mass. He said the book had been read by several inmates as it circulated through the prison.

In addition to his letter, the envelope contained a chapter he had written in a book titled *Chicken Soup for the Prisoner's Soul*. His piece was titled "The Healing Touch." It was a moving description of the first time his family came to visit him after his initial incarceration.

I learned from his writings that he would be spending the rest of his life in prison. This caught me completely off guard. The tone of his first letter did not seem to be that of a man convicted of murder. The voice I perceived was one of a regular guy, just a dad with a couple of young kids. He seemed to be a lot like me.

As a father, I imagined the sadness he must have felt when seeing his children through the Plexiglas partition that separated them from him. And I imagined how badly he must have felt knowing that the children he was supposed to be providing for were now the responsibility of his aging parents, who had to struggle just to stand up. I put myself in his place, in his shoes, sitting behind that glass wall and reaching out to touch the faces of my children, knowing that the barrier always would be there to prevent it. I imagined how much it must have touched his heart to read the words on his daughter's lips as she was about to leave: "Daddy, I love you. Everything will be okay."

What a heavy heart a father in prison must have. His burden can be lightened only by contact with his family, and by the empathy of those around him, and by the boundless mercy of God.

By mid-October Dale's predicament was back on my heart and mind. I felt that there was more to this man than he had initially revealed to me, so I wrote to him and asked if he would be willing to share his story. He replied a week later.

He said he had killed his wife, but it was an accident. The pistol went off when they were struggling for it during a heated argument over his infidelity. He said he was about to break off the affair with the other woman and insisted that he never would have killed his wife on purpose. But the jury didn't believe him, and the judge gave him a life sentence.

*Dear Chad:*

*...I remember sitting on the floor of a 10x10-foot cell on Easter Sunday of 1993. The sun was shining and spring was in the air. I should have been at Mass with my family. Instead I was one of 11 men crowded in a four-man cell. I slept on the floor in the corner viewing the blue sky and clouds through a filthy window. I prayed for God to bless my family and to do whatever He wanted with me.*

*My daughters were 10 and 12 years old when I began my incarceration. I realized that my wife would never see them graduate or get married because of me. Losing my personal freedom was nothing compared to what I had taken away from my wife's family and my children.*

*As I stepped off the bus into my new home, Angola State Prison, I prayed that God would watch over my family. My prayers would be answered and, in the midst of the bloodiest prison in America, He would choose to watch over me as well. I performed countless hours of labor by day and wrote endless letters to my daughters by night.*

*After a few years, I was given a job as the chap-*

lain's clerk at the main prison and would remain in that position for the next 12 years. Born and raised as a Catholic, learning to work with other denominations and faith groups was a new experience for me. I enrolled in a three-year course in Catholic Ministry and Theology. I hoped that my daughters could feel some pride in their father as I became one of the first 12 inmates to be commissioned as a Eucharistic Peer Minister.

One day I noticed an old man who had been locked up for over 40 years and had been working for six cents an hour. He was spending the few pennies he had feeding stray cats. When I asked why, he said, "Son, we're all in this together. We have to look after one another...even the cats!"

That was the moment I asked God for forgiveness and to use me as an instrument of faith. I prayed that He would make me the person He wanted me to be and the father I needed to be behind bars for my children. Prison had taught me how to forgive myself and others.

I believe that God uses people in our lives to bring into focus what is really important in life. For me that has become my family and my spiritual growth. I may never walk the earth as a free man again, but I know that Christ is using me to help others in their faith journey. I have met many people and read countless books over the years that have helped shape and mold me into the person I am today.

*Earlier this year, my spiritual advisor gave me the book entitled* Waiting for Eli.... *I've shared this book with several inmates here, and we have prayed for Eli and your family on many occasions at Mass. Although our community is small in numbers, these men continue to awe me with their compassion. During conversations, they continue to ask about baby Eli. Some have even echoed my own feelings, asking:*

*"Why? Why not inflict me, an outcast of society, and allow this little boy to have a normal, healthy life?"*

*My only conclusion is that God works in mysterious ways.*

*When I wrote to you initially, I mentioned the inmate who was moved to prayer for the first time in 30 years after reading your book. (By the way, his name is Fred.) I saw the hurt in his eyes for your family. I felt God's presence that night when we prayed the Lord's Prayer. Just as the old man who fed the cats that day in the yard moved me to ask God for his forgiveness and mercy, Fred's compassion for Eli reminded me that we are all in this together, one family in the body of Christ....*

*Thanks for sharing your family's story and life with me. We walk by faith and not by sight. The journey continues....*
*–Dale*

To me, Dale's testimony reveals the depths of God's

forgiveness and mercy. While Dale's suffering may be psychological and Eli's physical, God is using both of them in His own way to bring others back to Him.

In a conversation I had with one of my spiritual advisors, Father Manny Fernandez, I shared several of the ways I feel Eli's life has impacted others. He was interested to hear my report and responded with words of encouragement:

"Even if Eli never walks, God is using him to bring hope to the hopeless, and to heal the depressed. He is using your son and you. Don't stop sharing this story."

# Chapter 7

## *The peaks and valleys of life*

Everyone has days that he or she will never forget. These can be days in which we have a life-altering experience, or when we hear news that will affect our lives, or the lives of our loved ones, forever. I lived through two such days in January of 2010.

January 20 promised to be a long day at school. Ashley had taken off work to bring Eli to an appointment with his urologist. Eli was to undergo testing to determine whether he would have to be catheterized in order to avoid kidney damage and the frequent urinary tract infections that are common in children with *spina bifida*.

Ashley and I were worried. I hated the thought that catheterization might have to be a part of Eli's daily routine for the rest of his life.

For most of the day, I fretted over Eli's test results, despite the fact that the next day was the ceremony for the annual Teacher of the Year Awards for Lafayette Parish (county). I had been nominated earlier in the month and was a finalist in the inspirational teacher category. Because of this, my spirits should have been up. But they weren't.

So, as is my custom, I sought comfort and strength through prayer in our school's chapel.

When I got home after school, I found Ashley sitting quietly in our rocking chair and rocking Eli. I could tell she was holding back tears.

She proceeded to tell me that the news wasn't good. She said the urologist pointed out there were three options, including having a more thorough test done in six months. At that time it could be determined with certainty whether Eli had full or only partial use of his bladder – which would tell us for sure whether he had to be catheterized.

"We could have started cathing him now, this week, but I just wasn't ready," she said. "So, I scheduled the test for six months from now."

Hearing the disappointment and pain in my wife's voice and witnessing her raw emotions was hard to handle. Feeling defeated, I sat down on the couch and looked at the innocence in Eli's eyes as he smiled at us.

Eli has limited movement in his lower legs, especially his left, and we had no real idea to what extent he might have feeling below his waist. When he was six months old he cried when a needle was injected into his thigh during the first of a set of shots. But he showed no evidence of feeling when the second round was injected. The absence of feeling below his waist would be to his benefit when the process of catheterization was eventually begun – if, in fact, he would have to be catheterized.

But, one way or the other, I knew Eli would have lifelong problems with incontinence. As his father, it hurts me to know that I cannot give him comfort or guidance in regard to some of the problems he will encounter as an adult and that there are certain things that he will not be able to experience.

I sat on the couch and cried as I looked at my son.

Ashley placed Eli on the floor and extended her hand to me. I took it and got up from the couch, and we hugged.

"I'm sorry. I know how much you wanted to hear that he did not need this. Try not to focus totally on this. You deserve to have a good time tomorrow night," she whispered as she held me.

\* \* \* \* \*

The next day, work went by rather quickly. I wasn't really excited or nervous about the award event that evening; really, I was honored just to be recognized and wanted to represent my school well. Even though I didn't think my name would be called, I like to be prepared so I did jot down a little something to say, just in case.

I prayed for the right words and even began looking through the Bible for something appropriate. But nothing was coming to me. Then I remembered a card with a famous quote by Jesuit Fr. Pedro Arrupe, a card I obtained at a recent faculty retreat. I located it, folded it, and put it in my pocket.

Arriving at the awards ceremony venue, the Heymann Performing Arts Center, with my beautiful wife, I could see many supporters, faculty members, parents and friends waiting to greet the honorees. In all, 16 teachers were nominated in four categories. About 45 minutes into the program, it was time to announce the top finalist in the inspirational teacher category. Each educator was recognized individually, then the announcer opened the envelope and started reading.

Turns out, the name he called was mine.

Momentarily stunned, I walked over to the podium, took the award in my left hand, and firmly shook the hand of the presenter. Fighting back all the emotion of the past few days and months, I reached into my pocket and pulled out Fr. Arrupe's famous words:

> *Nothing is more practical than finding God, that is, than falling in love in a quite absolute, final way.*
> *What you are in love with, what seizes your imagination, will affect everything. It will decide what will get you out of bed in the mornings, what you will*

*do with your evenings, how you spend your weekends, what you read, who you know, what breaks your heart, and what amazes you with joy and gratitude.*

*Fall in love, stay in love, and it will decide everything.*

When I finished the reading, I expressed my love and gratitude to my family, students, friends and colleagues. Holding the award high, I concluded by saying, "St. Thomas More, this one's for you!"

As I headed back toward my seat, my eyes glimpsed the beauty of my wife's smile, and I saw that she was on the verge of tears.

That night was not so much about me as a teacher or what I had done in my classroom. Rather, it was about an omnipotent God, a special-needs child, and the extraordinary school community of which I am proud to be a part.

# Chapter 8

# *Surrendering to God's will*

I could feel the pull of the wind on my car as I drove westward down the interstate from Lafayette to nearby Crowley, praying silently as I prepared to present Eli's story at Notre Dame High School. It was a beautiful day in February of 2010, and there was not a cloud in the sky.

I was following my friend, Lance Strother, whose band was scheduled to play before and after my talk. He and I were close, not only because we worked in campus ministry together but also because we were members of the same men's prayer group. I always appreciated his musical talent and his passion for sharing the Gospel with our students.

When we got to the school, we set up our equipment in the gymnasium. I hooked up my laptop and projector for my PowerPoint presentation; he and fellow band members connected their musical instruments to their sound system.

Before the crowd arrived I prayed with Lance and the band that we'd be successful in reaching the students, in touching their hearts and minds. The band played a few songs as the students filed in following a pro-life march across town. It was Pro-Life Day at Notre Dame High. The gym filled up with about 600 students, parents, faculty and townspeople.

Right before the emcee turned the program over to me I requested that Lance play a certain song he wrote called "Totally Falling." I sat on the edge of the stage facing the student body and sang along. Lance's song is about recognizing that at some point in our lives people of faith come to a place where we surrender our will to God's will: "Thy will be done" becomes our mantra. As for me, I had gradually come to accept the fact that God had a vision for Eli's life that was different from mine; it was at this point that I experienced the most significant spiritual growth of my life – when I surrendered my will to His. The lyrics of the music spoke to me, and I prayed that they spoke to the audience as well.

Before I began my talk, Lance introduced me to the crowd. They welcomed me politely then listened closely. In fact, from the moment I began speaking till the moment I finished, you could have heard a pin drop. A moving image of Eli and Ephraim was fixed on the screen as I concluded the presentation.

Eli's story left a mark there that day, but it would be six months before I came to fully understand how much of a mark it was.

The following August, I received an e-mail from a student named Brittany Domingue, who had been in attendance that day. She had read *Waiting for Eli* over the summer and felt moved to tell me of her reaction to the book.

*Dear Mr. Judice,*

*I just wanted to let you know how inspiring your son's story is for me!*

*My name is Brittany and I attend Notre Dame High School. I was a freshman when you told Eli's story at our Pro-Life Day gathering.*

*As you were telling your story, I was holding back tears. I thought the faith you have in the Lord is just amazing! When you were finished giving your testimony, I was one of the many in line to give you a hug and tell you how happy I was that your son was doing good.*

*I didn't realize then the true importance of Eli's miraculous purpose. I understood that all of those miracles were by God's grace alone and that without all the faith and prayers of you, your wife, friends, and family that Eli may not have turned out the way he did.*

*I didn't realize how much of an impact this story*

*had on me until I finished reading your book.*

*While I was reading I remembered some things I had forgotten. I have three very good friends who all have a parent recently diagnosed with cancer. Two were diagnosed before I heard your testimony at Notre Dame and one after. I always prayed for them! It hurt me to see my close friends watch their parents go through that. I know it tore them apart inside.*

*It wasn't until after I heard little Eli's story that I realized I was barely trying. I was going through the motions, not reaching my full prayer potential. I remember thinking,* If little Eli could make it through this with the prayers of loved ones and friends then they (my friends' parents) can make it through this with our prayers also! *After that I prayed with new hope and intensity. After a very long time we received the good news that two of the parents had finished chemo and were considered to be cancer-free, and one of them is just recently starting to get better – which is amazing considering the condition he was in.*

*I found that, because of Eli's story, I prayed with the thought that if God could help him like this then He could do anything; He could cure my friends' family, and He has. This may not seem like much to some, but it means a lot to me.*

*Father Matthew Higginbotham gave my mom your book,* Waiting for Eli. *She read it in a matter of hours and cried the whole time. She thought it was absolutely beautiful.*

Once she finished it, I borrowed the book. The story came alive to me again! It's been three days since I finished it and I can't get the beautiful story out of my mind....

I have been going through a tough time this year and have gotten a lot closer to my faith. I attended the retreat "Steubenville on the Bayou" in Houma-Thibodaux. It was the most spiritual weekend of my life. That Friday night they asked, for those who would like, to please stand up and receive a personal blessing. Before I realized what was even happening, I was standing up and walking to the front to get the blessing. I honestly believe the Holy Spirit was with me because it's not like me to do that kind of thing. I also felt an amazing peace the whole time.

... Eli has given me the courage to live my life for God. This letter is kind of my way of making the way I feel, and what I want to do, official for me!

This story has changed my life, and I just wanted to share that with you and your family!

Your family is always in my prayers. Thank you again.

–Brittany Domingue

# Chapter 9

## *Angels among us*

At the beginning of the summer of 2010, when Eli was a year and four months old, Ashley and I took him and his brother on a vacation so they could enjoy the white sand and blue water of Destin, Florida.

The boys had a blast, splashing around in the pool and sometimes in the surf, as seagulls circled overhead and children of all ages played noisily nearby. Ashley and I took turns wading into the shallow water while holding Eli.

While in Destin, we noticed some white discharge on the front of Eli's diapers, but we were not sure what it was. He appeared to be feeling fine and having a great time.

Shortly after our return home, we took his temperature and saw that he had a high fever. We were concerned that it might be a malfunction of his shunt – the device that had been surgically implanted in his head right after his birth to allow neural fluids to flow up and down his spinal cord at a normal rate. So, I brought him to the doctor. Ashley couldn't accompany us because she had to work.

It turned out that the shunt was not the issue. The doctor ordered a urine sample to test for bacteria. If the test came back positive, it meant that Eli had a urinary tract infection.

These infections are common among children with *spina bifida*; they can be avoided by not allowing urine to linger in the bladder. Individuals with Eli's condition often require assistance in emptying the bladder through the use of catheterization. We were aware of this possibility but were praying Eli would be the exception to the rule; we were hoping he would be able to empty his bladder with the aid of medication. But that prospect was fading fast.

The nurses carefully laid Eli on the cold mat on the examining table, with the lower half of his body exposed. They were preparing to catheterize him to obtain the urine sample.

I turned away from them and looked the opposite way, facing the wall, with tears streaming down my face. It was surreal to hope Eli would scream, indicating he had feeling below the waist, while at the same time wanting to hear no scream, which would tell me he was in no pain. But he did scream. Then he cried loudly.

Hearing that, experiencing it, I didn't know if his screams were from pain or fear and anxiety. It was a reaction that was to be expected from a child his age in a strange place surrounded by strangers probing the private parts of his body. When I realized they had begun to catheterize him, it felt like my stomach came up into my throat, and I cried out loud as Eli cried and screamed.

The test came back positive, confirming that Eli did indeed have the first urinary tract infection of his life. It would have to be treated with antibiotics.

Driving home afterward and watching him in the rearview mirror, I knew the only thing that was going to get our family through this emotionally trying time was prayer. I resolved then and there that I would pray every day – and pray hard – for God's mercy.

A few days after the harrowing experience in the doctor's office, I received an e-mail from a teacher whom I had met earlier in the year while giving a presentation at a Catholic high school in Morgan City, a town about an hour and a half southeast of Lafayette. When I was there she told me she was totally inspired by Eli's story. I felt an immediate and strong connection to her, partly because we were both Catholic high school teachers. Needless to say, I was very happy to see her e-mail.

Chad,

...When you came to speak to our school a couple of months ago, I was overwhelmed and touched by Eli's story. Your family's faith and hope in such a difficult time was truly inspiring. When you came to my class, I purchased your book and read it in one sitting.

This week your book has become our miracle. It has already given our family so much direction and many signs. Early Monday morning my brother-in-law (my husband's brother) and his wife gave birth to a beautiful baby girl, Lillian Claire Autrey. She appeared to be very alert and healthy.

My husband is an emergency room nurse at the hospital where the baby was born, and later that night while he was on duty he called me unexpectedly and said:

"Sarah, go get my mom and sister and come to the hospital immediately."

Upon arrival, we were informed that the baby's breathing had become labored and she had been placed on a ventilator.

A few hours later, her lungs were not functioning well, her blood sugar had dropped drastically, her blood pressure was low, and it appeared one side of her heart was enlarged. We were beside ourselves.

The transport team had to rush her to Women's & Children's Hospital in Lafayette. On the way

out of town, I gave my husband your book and insisted that he have his brother read it.

That evening the baby was tested for Group B
strep – a form of bacteria all mothers are tested for
in pregnancy. Although her mother had tested nega-
tive, the baby had it. It was infecting her entire body,
and doctors discovered she also had pneumonia.

The following Tuesday an ultrasound revealed
that a portion of her brain, the corpus callosum,
may also be missing. An MRI or CT scan couldn't
be conducted to confirm this because she wasn't
stable enough to be moved. The pediatric neurologist
is unsure what long-term damage she may have. It
could be anything from minor to severe.

Wednesday her oxygen levels dropped dangerously
low, and the nurses were bagging her on the vent.
We had a priest called in and had her baptized. We
thought it was only a matter of time until they came
to tell us she was gone. After the baptism, they decided to put her on an oscillating ventilator to see if this
improved her breathing. She is still in critical condition while taking medicine for her blood pressure,
plus morphine, antibiotics, and several other things.
They are telling us she is the most critical baby back
there right now, but we will not stop praying.

My brother-in-law has been so touched by your
book, and we truly feel we are surrounded by you,
your wife, Ephraim and Eli. We were walking to
the NICU and noticed all of the precious fish on

*the wall with the names of children and their dates of birth. The one that caught my eye had your oldest son's name on it, Ephraim Judice. I knew it was another sign from above!*

*We are leaving soon to head back to Lafayette for the weekend to be with them. We have been praying for a miracle for the baby. I know they happen. You know they happen.*

*I know you are a very busy man, and between school, your family, and your testimony I know you are probably limited on time. However, if there is any way you could possibly speak to our family or come and pray with us for a moment, it would mean so much. Sharing your faith with my brother-in-law would mean so much....*

*...Thank you for anything you could do, and thank you for sharing such an inspirational story.*

*God bless you and your family,*
*Sarah Autrey*

I read her e-mail then called her right away to say, yes, I'd love to come to the hospital and pray with her and her family.

The following morning, I drove to Women's & Children's. I had butterflies in my stomach as I entered the building and made my way to the elevator. I was going to pray with a family I had never met, except for Sarah. A few years earlier I didn't even talk about faith in public out of concern for offending others. Things were very different now.

I found Sarah and her family in the waiting room of the Neonatal Intensive Care Unit. We hugged, and she introduced me to her husband and some members of her immediate family. After exchanging a few introductions and a little conversation, we settled down and prayed the rosary. Afterward, I visited briefly with the baby's father and even got to see the baby in her incubator.

Then I invited the family – a bunch of Sarah's husband's brothers and sisters and a slew of their kids – to come to our home to meet my boys and my parents. They readily accepted and followed me home in three vehicles. They had met Ashley earlier that day; she was on duty at Women's & Children's in the NICU.

Ephraim was so excited to have other kids his age to play with that he was beside himself. Some of the younger children sat on the floor and interacted with Eli, and the adults took turns holding him. With each smile and twinkle in Eli's eyes, I could see by the expression on our adult visitors' faces that God was sending them a reaffirming message: Don't give up!

The following morning, Sarah sent me another e-mail:

> *Chad,*
> *...My niece has continued to get stronger since we*

*met with you and your family, and she may even be*
*coming home next week. Yesterday her brain issues*
*were confirmed through an MRI. A small piece of*
*her brain is missing, and it is not clear how this will*
*affect her development. She is also having seizures,*
*has some sort of optic nerve condition, and her vision*
*may be slightly impaired or she could be legally blind.*

*...Eli's story continues to give hope to our family.*
*We left several of your books in the NICU for other*
*parents and family members of patients to read for*
*comfort and direction. Last night, after the results*
*from her MRI came back, my father-in-law said:*
*"She needs our prayers more than ever. She may be*
*our Eli."*

*– Sarah Autrey*

Sarah wrote me again three or four months after
our visit. She said that her niece was home and doing better than expected despite having to deal with
multiple physical challenges each day.

A story she shared confirmed to me that God puts
these angels such as Eli and Lillian Claire among us
as a constant reminder that although they cannot do
all of the physical things other children can, they can
do something other children can't.

*My niece was in the NICU for two months. Al-*
*though she came home on a feeding tube and nu-*
*merous medications, she has been such a blessing to*

all of us. Her infectious giggle and smile can make anyone's day better. Doctors say she has limited blood flow to her optic nerves, which more or less means she cannot see.

Upon my return to school this year, I shared with my students why I thought God had brought Eli's story to Central Catholic. I also told them about the blessing your family was to ours this past summer. They were amazed at the way God had brought me back in touch with you.

One night after sharing this story with my students, I was walking down my street with my niece, Lillian Claire, in her stroller. I stopped at a home where a colleague of mine lives. I am teaching her daughter, who was overwhelmed to meet the little girl she had prayed so hard for. The following day at school she approached me, saying she had been thinking about my niece.... She told me that if she could sacrifice her eyesight so my niece could see, she would do it. My student is an amazing young woman, but this statement just blew me away. We can tell people a million times that we are praying for them and that we want their loved one to get better, but to say it that way was truly touching. Moved to tears, I hugged my student and told her I love her. Her words were so sincere and simple, yet so profound.

Moments such as these are when I know God moves in these children; this is when I know He speaks to us through them.

– Sarah Autrey

# Chapter 10

# *The news we prayed we'd never hear*

My hand slammed down on the alarm clock on the end table next to my bed. It was half past four in the morning. I hadn't woken up that early since school let out a month earlier. It was the second week in July 2010.

We were going to New Orleans to bring Eli to Children's Hospital for diagnostic testing of his ability to urinate on his own. It's the test Ashley scheduled six months earlier, the definitive test that would determine once and for all whether Eli would have to be catheterized. Ephraim had spent the night at my parents' house, and Ashley's mom was going with us to New Orleans.

After arriving just in time for the appointment, we sat in the waiting room for about ten minutes before a nurse called Eli's name. Ashley got up to bring him and suggested I remain in the waiting room with her mom. Nodding at Ashley, I watched Eli reaching back over her shoulder and looking at me as they disappeared behind the swinging doors.

The test that was to be conducted required him to be catheterized and to have fluid injected into his bladder. The test would determine the level of pressure in his bladder before urination. The level of pressure, in turn, would tell us whether he had the ability to empty his bladder on his own or whether he would need catheterization to do so.

After about 20 minutes, Ashley and Eli emerged from the testing area and returned to the waiting room. With a smile on her face, Ashley looked at us and said, "We're done. Let's go."

Walking back to the car, I was relieved that the initial testing was behind us, but I knew it would be a long week waiting for the results. Ashley shared some encouraging news on our return trip to Lafayette. While running the test, a nurse said she suspected the doctor might try to control Eli's bladder function with medication. Although the nurse's observation was encouraging, I didn't want to get my hopes up until I heard it from the doctor himself.

Well, when we did hear from the doctor the following week, the news was not good. Eli's test showed that his bladder did not function properly. This increased the risk of kidney damage and frequent urinary tract infections. To avoid these medical problems in the future, Eli would have to be catheterized five times a day while also taking medication.

I wishfully asked the doctor if he had ever had a patient who had to be catheterized only temporarily.

"No, this is normally permanent," he responded.

Leaving the building, Ashley was holding Eli and looking back at me. Tears were falling from her eyes and from mine.

"At least we are not wondering anymore how it is going to be," she said as her voice cracked.

I could not respond. I was just trying to hold myself together emotionally as we walked toward the car.

A few days later, Ashley and I and our parents attended classes to learn how to properly catheterize our boy. Though Ashley was qualified to teach us, she felt more comfortable having someone else do it.

And so we began catheterizing Eli five times a day. I had a very difficult time with it. I felt depressed, defeated, maybe even abandoned by God. I kept telling myself I could do this, but deep down I could hardly believe we were having to do it. I kept thinking, *There just must be some other way.* And, at the same time, I knew that if Eli was ever going to accept this as part of his life, I was going to have to resign myself to it as well.

# Chapter 11

## *Eli's mentor*

Whoever said the darkest hour is just before dawn really knew what he or she was talking about.

During the dark and difficult time when we learned we would have to catheterize Eli, I received an e-mail that totally and immediately lifted my spirits and re-built my hope for Eli's future. It was like a message from above, but it was written on a computer keyboard by a young man with *spina bifida*.

> *Dear Mr. Judice*
>
> *My name is Jonathan Cunningham. I was in the graduating class of 2005 from St. Thomas More. I recently read an article about you and your wife coming to the realization that you were going to have a*

child born with spina bifida. *I can't say that I have any experience with being the parent of a child born with a birth defect, but I do have a lot of experience living with a birth defect. I was born with* spina bifida.

*I am 24 now, and although my life is different from the average person, it is still very rich, productive and rewarding. While this hasn't always been the case, I am now at a place in my life where I am able to see that nothing in God's world happens by mistake.*

*This birth defect has never stopped me from doing anything I wanted to do. Even though most people usually make a quick judgment about my physical abilities, after getting to know me they quickly realize their stereotype was misguided.*

*I just wanted to make sure you knew that there are other people in the area who are dealing with similar situations. If I can be of service to you or your family, please let me know.*

*Sincerely,*

*Jon Cunningham*

I quickly hit the reply button and responded to Jonathan's message. I thanked him for contacting me and told him I'd like to meet with him in the near future. I pointed out that I recognized his name, that one of my colleagues had mentioned him to me more than once since Eli was born and suggested that I should make an effort to get to know him.

A few days after receiving his first e-mail, I got a second.

> Mr. Judice,
>
> I just finished reading your book. I am not much of a reader and was very surprised how caught up in the book I became after reading the first paragraph. It was a moving testimony of how, when faced with the unexpected, God is always there and gives us all we need when we seek His guidance.
>
> ...My mother was not aware of my condition until after my birth, and she was told that I would probably never walk. The doctor couldn't have been more wrong. Most of the time I walk with crutches but I am able to walk without them as well.... I have had surgery many times in my life.
>
> Eli is truly blessed for his body to function at such a high level despite the birth defect. That is the power of God....
>
> I would love to meet you and your family at some point. I live in Baton Rouge now but I am in Lafayette often. Hope to hear from you soon....
>
> Sincerely,
> Jon Cunningham

I responded by inviting Jonathan to our house the next time he was in town. I told him about Eli's test results and asked if he'd be willing to talk with us about his own experiences with things such as catheterization. I had been hoping that one day Eli would have someone he could talk with who truly understood what he was going through, someone who was walking the same path in life. I wanted Jonathan to know that he had given our family hope for Eli, hope in a world that is so full of pessimism and negativity.

I felt Jonathan just might be the perfect mentor for Eli – as well as for Ashley and me.

Four or five days after receiving that second e-mail from Jonathan, I watched as this young man with *spina bifida* walked with crutches to our front door after having driven himself to our home. Needless to say, I felt a strong and immediate connection to him.

He shared some of his experiences growing up with his condition and how important his family had been to him. Jonathan was open and honest about all of the physical, psychological and emotional challenges he faced on his journey. We learned that he had 13 surgeries in his life, all of which were necessary to become a full-functioning independent adult.

Jonathan has visited with us several times, and our relationship has gotten stronger each time. He has become a steady, true mentor not only to Eli but to our entire family. It would be safe to say he's now like one of our family.

# Chapter 12

# *Choosing life*

Since the release of *Waiting for Eli*, I have continued to hear stories of mothers-in-waiting who read the book and were influenced by it in their decisions to reject abortion and to carry their babies to term.

One of these women is a nurse who works with my wife Ashley in the neonatal care unit of Women's & Children's Hospital in Lafayette. Another was a teenager when she got pregnant and is now a college student studying to be a neonatal nurse.

The first account involves a couple named Tracey and Jason Hargrave, who were expecting their second child. Tracey began experiencing abdominal pains so severe that she had to be hospitalized. She was tested for a certain virus that if contracted during pregnancy could result in the baby suffering from hearing loss, partial loss of eyesight and an array of mental disabilities. Unfortunately, the test came back positive.

A few months later, Ashley invited Tracey and Jason to a presentation I was making in the nearby town of Carencro. After my talk, I was signing copies of my book when a couple I hadn't met before walked up to me. Before they said a word, I figured they must be Tracey and Jason.

"Are you Tracey?" I asked.

"Yes, and this is my husband, Jason," she responded as her eyes began filling with tears.

When I shook hands with Jason, I could see the anguish on his face. I knew what he was going through. I chatted with the Hargraves for a minute, then both of them bought a copy of the book. Neither wanted to wait till the other finished reading it.

"We're praying for you and your baby," I said as they moved away from the signing table and headed for the door.

Two months later, I learned that following the presentation in Carencro, Tracey and her husband sat in their vehicle, unable to speak to one another for a while. They had come to a decision a few days earlier to terminate the pregnancy, based on the test results.

"We both sat there, unable to look at one another. Through tears, I told Jason, 'I cannot do this.' He said he could not either," she recalled.

"It was at that moment that we decided to keep our child, regardless of the way it was being sent to us. We felt a peace that night that had such a calming effect that I cannot describe it.

"The Monday after your presentation we went in for another ultrasound, and it was then that we discovered that our child no longer had a heartbeat. When I asked the doctor when the baby's life had ended, the timetable I was given put it on the very same night we had heard your presentation.

"I know God showed us mercy that evening after we made that decision not to give up on our baby. My doctor said that in her 30 years of practicing medicine she had never seen a pregnancy such as this end in a miscarriage.

"The pain of losing my child was unbearable, but at least I have closure knowing I will not have to live with the guilt that would have been there if I had had a hand in ending her life."

Tracey and Jason named their baby girl Bethany.

\* \* \* \* \*

Camryn Hayes was another expectant mother whose decision to reject abortion was influenced by the message of hope in *Waiting for Eli*. She was 18 when she became pregnant.

A senior at the high school in Church Point, about 45 minutes northwest of Lafayette, Camryn was in shock when she learned of the pregnancy. So was the baby's father, Kyle Carmello. They were in even greater shock when they went to a doctor's appointment and got the results of a test showing the baby was afflicted with a condition known as anencephaly and had no chance of surviving, according to the statistics from medical science.

Camryn recalled the doctor's speaking to her in a blunt, businesslike manner.

"This condition is 100 percent fatal," he said. "Your child will not live."

"You need to decide what you would like to do, and your decision must be made before 22 weeks in the state of Louisiana. I know a good doctor in Houston who can perform an abortion for you."

Camryn and Kyle left the doctor's office scared, offended and somewhat confused.

It was just about a week after this encounter with the doctor that a copy of my book found its way into Camryn's hands. She found solace and hope in what she read, partly because of the book's pro-life message. So, she passed it on to Kyle and to members of her family.

The book stimulated a sense of optimism and a newfound hope for the future, hope that somehow things would turn out all right. Camryn and her loved ones decided to pray for a miracle for the unborn baby. As I and my family had done for Eli, they prayed for the intercession of Blessed Father Seelos and Charlene Richard, "The Little Cajun Saint," who is buried in the tiny community of Richard, just a few miles from their hometown. And they started attending Mass every Thursday at the little church near Charlene's grave.

A month after reading the book and beginning a focused prayer regimen, Camryn, Kyle and Camryn's mom returned to see the doctor.

"So what's the plan?" the doctor asked.

"There is no plan. I am carrying the baby to term," Camryn responded.

"Please understand, your child will not survive," the doctor said emphatically. "It has no skull. It has absolutely no chance of survival."

Camryn became angry.

"I don't want to hear this," she said. "We are living on faith."

"I'm not going to argue with The Man Upstairs, but if you jump off a 50-foot building, do you think you will live?" the doctor asked.

Now, Kyle was angry.

"That's enough!" Kyle said. "We're leaving."

Camryn remained faithful to her word to carry the baby to term and to keep on praying for the best.

The baby was born in July of 2011 and died upon delivery. He was buried in Richard, one row away from Charlene's grave.

The impact the baby's life had on his parents and their families is well-described in what Camryn wrote shortly after his death.

> *Valentine's Day will never be the same....*
>
> *One phone call informing me of "questionable" test results was the beginning of the unimaginable for me. Many of my friends and family tried to reassure me. After all, most positive results eventually came back as "false positives," right?*
>
> *As much as I wanted to believe it, deep down I knew something was wrong. I just had that feeling.*
>
> *The doctor's words will haunt me for the rest of my life. My entire body went numb. All I could do was cry and ask, "What do I do?" At 18 years old, I never could have dreamed of being faced with a decision like this. I was so afraid.*
>
> *The doctor answered my question with a simple solution: Have an abortion.*
>
> *Two days later, a friend loaned me the book* Waiting for Eli: A Father's Journey from Fear to Faith.... *Eli's story gave me hope and belief that a miracle could happen for my angel. And from that point on I decided to choose faith over fear.*
>
> *The most significant sign I received was after praying to feel my baby move, and before going to bed one night, I felt him move for the very first time.*
>
> *From that moment on and to this day, I would sacrifice all the sleepless nights, aches and pains just to feel him move again. I have found peace knowing that he was always safe within me.*
>
> *What began as a horrifying journey on February*

*14, 2011, came to a peaceful end on July 10, 2011. London Dre Carmello became an angel in heaven that day.*

*And though he took my entire heart, I know that my love went with him.*

*His life continues through all who have come to a new or better understanding of our loving God and His plans for us. It is my hope that others will recognize this beautiful miracle, and make the choice to always give life.*

Camryn graduated from high school in May of 2011 and went on to study nursing at Louisiana State University at Eunice. She said her fondest hope is that God will work through her, as a neonatal nurse, to give every child - regardless of its condition at birth - the chance to live its life to the fullest, whatever God wills that to be.

# Chapter 13

# *An adoption that was meant to be*

E li's story has touched the hearts of people far and wide, but some of the most poignant examples have occurred in my own back yard, as it were. Just up Interstate 49, an hour or so north of Lafayette, is the town of Bunkie, the home of Samantha and Bobby LaHaye and their adopted daughter, Aubrey, a beautiful child born with Down syndrome.

Now, in the world of adoption, prospective parents generally don't have their hearts set on adopting a special-needs baby. But that sentiment has been known to change the moment they meet the child.

Such was the case with Samantha and Aubrey when the angelic blonde baby was first held by the woman whose heart she would steal.

I met Samantha soon after she had read *Waiting*

*for Eli*, and she said the book reinforced her decision to adopt Aubrey.

She explained that she and her husband were unable to have children and were thinking about adopting. She was employed by a public school system and worked with blind and visually impaired children.

One day, while making routine house calls to visit a visually impaired child in foster care, she met Aubrey. The child was in the care of Mr. and Mrs. Joseph Chevis, who were the foster parents of several children.

Entering the home, Samantha saw Mrs. Chevis rocking a baby girl. They talked and Samantha learned that the child, besides having Down syndrome and visual impairment, had a heart condition that would require corrective surgery six months later. When Aubrey was two weeks old, her biological parents realized they were unable to provide the care she needed, so they gave her up for adoption. The Chevis family had nurtured and cared for Aubrey through most of the first year of her life.

Mrs. Chevis asked Samantha if she'd like to hold Aubrey, and Samantha readily agreed to do so. Truth is, Samantha fell in love with the child the moment she laid eyes on her.

Mrs. Chevis saw the loving way Samantha held the baby and the way she looked at her. Then she said something that was very insightful, if not prophetic:

"I knew you were coming. I knew this baby had a mother and that she was coming."

The lady couldn't have been more right.

Besides Mrs. Chevis's observation, there were other signs that this was the baby for Samantha and Bobby: Aubrey's features strongly resembled those of Samantha's mother, and Bobby's great-grandfather happened to be named Aubrey.

Samantha was absolutely smitten by the child. Sunday visits soon developed into long sleepovers and lots of quality time spent with the little girl. As the bond strengthened, so did the idea of becoming Aubrey's foster parents. Even more than that, the LaHayes were considering adopting Aubrey and making her a full-fledged member of their family.

However, the prospective parents understood that adopting Aubrey would mean a lifelong commitment of sacrifice and perseverance. They were aware of this because Sam's grandfather had a special-needs sibling. This caused them to hesitate and to think harder about whether they could handle such a responsibility.

This is the point at which Samantha got ahold of my book. But she was particularly affected by the Scriptural passage on the bookmark I had placed in this and most of the books I autograph. It's from the Gospel of Matthew:

> *Amen, I say to you, unless you turn and become like this child, you will not enter the kingdom of*

*heaven. Whoever humbles himself like this child is the greatest in the kingdom of heaven. And whoever receives one child such as this in my name receives me.*

"I prayed that prayer every day and night, and I truly believe in it," she told me.

She also said she read the book in just two days.

"Bobby would come into our room to check on me periodically and to ask if I was okay. I would just nod my head slowly up and down as tears rolled down my cheeks," she said.

"It was amazing! What I was reading and the feelings I was having about Aubrey and our situation, they seemed to be the same ones you were talking about with your son.

"When I read about Blessed Father Seelos it just reinforced the feelings I was having. I cried even more. Bobby's grandmother had just given me one of Father Seelos' prayer cards.... When reading what you wrote about your visit to his shrine, I knew I had to go there someday to pray, that I was destined to do that."

Samantha then pointed out that she had come across a Saint Therese prayer card which bore a prayer for guidance in motherhood. She took that as another sign.

"Both shocked and amazed, I started thinking about what you kept talking about in your book – about things happening that would appear to be mere coincidences but through the eyes of faith are all signs from God.

"So, your book opened my eyes and helped me through the journey to foster and adopt our beautiful daughter. Thank you for sharing Eli's story; God has used it to change the lives of so many, but especially our family's," she said.

The LaHayes officially adopted Aubrey two days after her second birthday. Even the usually stoic and expressionless judge became rather emotional at the triumphant moment when the adoption was finalized.

# Chapter 14

## *Bringing men to prayer*

I t's a statistical fact of life these days that more women in the U.S. go to church and synagogue regularly than men. Women are known to pray more frequently and – I'll go out on a limb here – perhaps even in a more heartfelt manner, generally speaking.

I know this may sound like gross generalizations, but, as Herman Melville once said, "Truth uncompromisingly told will always have its jagged edges."

Further anecdotal evidence of the truth of what I'm saying can be observed readily in our part of the country when women and children attend church services while men sometimes just wait in the car listening to a football game.

Thus, I found it especially gratifying to learn about several men who sought to improve their prayer life and deepen their faith after being inspired by Eli's story.

These stories came to my attention in the form of letters from people who had read *Waiting for Eli*. Here's what two of them had to say:

Coach Judice,

... I went home the night I heard you speak and asked my boyfriend what his greatest fear was. To my surprise, he gave the same answer you did. (To have a physically or mentally handicapped child.) This opened the floor for much discussion. I shared with him the experience I had that night when you shared Eli's story with our sorority. He was not raised with faith in his life, but he has always wanted more.

The next day, he came home with three books. One was a book of prayers, the second was a book describing the Catholic Mass, and the third was Waiting for Eli.

He admits he has never finished a book in his life. But he wants yours to be his first.

When I asked him why he bought these books, he said that he needs to start praying for his future – not so much for himself, but for his future wife and kids.

In the past month, a person who has always had excuses for not going to Mass on Sunday has not missed one. Not only does he go, but he leaves talking about how our priest has provided insight for him to begin to change things in his life – and receive the *grace to see little things that God has meant for us to see and appreciate.*

*...Look how much God has used your family to change his life for the better. Eli got one more person to believe in the power of God and miracles.... I pray for your family every night.*

*Know that your son is making a difference in many people's lives.*

*Sincerely,*

*Tiffany Landry*

Chad:

*I am an '86 graduate of St. Thomas More High School who received your book from my 12-year-old daughter for Christmas. To say I was moved by the book is a tremendous understatement.*

*I couldn't help but draw some parallels from the situation my wife and I were in six years ago. However, I was nowhere near as resilient as you....*

*As I began reading your book, all those prior feelings rushed back to me and I had to put it down. I* walked away and thought, I will not be able to read this book because it is hitting too close to home. *However, I was drawn to read it and once I started again I couldn't put it down.*

*Although I have been a "Catholic" my entire life, I have been a fair-weather Catholic in recent years. I attended church regularly but I was all too often just going through the motions, thinking of what I had to* do next and not savoring the moment.

Your book has changed all that.

I have realized that I am very blessed with a wonderful wife and children. And that although I have put way too much importance on materialistic ideals, there is still time to change and focus on what is really important. Your realization that all happens with God's will, not ours, really hit home with me and put it all in proper perspective.

Thanks to your book, I am re-energized with giving my entire life to Jesus Christ and letting him guide me through life – instead of thinking I need to steer my ship. Prior to reading your book, I fear that my life was on a lonely path, but all that has changed now....

In summation, "thank you" sounds too light for all that I have received from this story. But thank you, your family and Eli for showing me the light and the path.

Kind Regards,
Craig G. Duplechin

# Chapter 15

# *The Twilight Zone*

I n April of 2011, in the week before Easter, Ashley and I and our boys took a trip to College Station, Texas. I had a speaking engagement at Texas A&M to share Eli's story with a group of students.

In the days leading up to the trip, Eli had been in a very irritable mood and had not been sleeping well. So, while in Texas, we had him examined at a walk-in clinic to check for common childhood illnesses. The doctor found nothing in particular about which to be alarmed.

After returning home, Eli continued to show symptoms that concerned us: He was lethargic, wasn't eating well, and just didn't seem to be himself.

Ashley and I suspected a malfunction of his shunt.

So, we took him to the doctor in Lafayette and had an MRI test run on him. It revealed a slight accumulation of fluid in the ventricles in his brain, but this did not appear to be much different from the results of an MRI he had a few months earlier.

Still, we were not convinced he was okay, so the following day Ashley brought him to see his neurologist at Tulane Medical Center in New Orleans. Ashley and Eli stayed in the hospital overnight, and the next day the doctor was able to adjust the magnetic setting on Eli's shunt. After that, it seemed to be functioning properly, so the doctor released them and they returned home.

It was now Holy Week, leading up to Easter Sunday. Around our house, things seemed to be getting back to normal. Good Friday was an especially good day. While being held by Ashley, Eli played in the wading pool in our back yard with his brother and two cousins.

I remember sitting back and starting to relax on the patio as I watched the kids having fun in the pool. I was really looking forward to some time off from school to re-energize myself before finishing the last bit of the school year. I had spoken more than 30 times during the previous seven or eight months, traveling around the state, promoting my book, telling Eli's story. I was pretty well burned out.

Early the next morning, I walked down the hall to get Eli out of bed and bring him into the den to

*Chad and Ashley Judice with sons*
*Ephraim (left) and Eli, at Christmastime 2011*

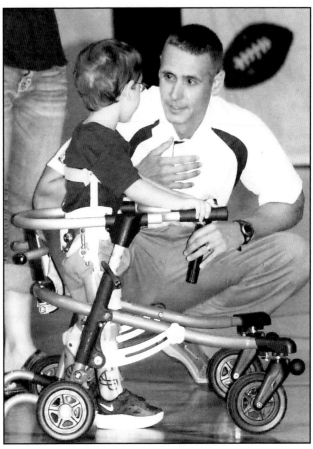

*Eli and I have a little chat following my presentation to a group in Ville Platte, La., in September of 2012. The crowd seemed to enjoy my talk, but they really loved it when Eli made an appearance afterward. There wasn't a dry eye in the place, including mine, when the little celebrity showed up.*

***Mother and child*** – *Ashley holds Eli during a hospital visit in February of 2012. We were at Tulane University Medical Center in New Orleans and Eli was being tested for a possible shunt malfunction.*

***Eli and friends –***
*Clockwise, starting
with photo above: Eli
with mentor Jonathan
Cunningham; Chris
Brewster, a high school
student who survived a
brain tumor; Eli with his
big brother, Ephraim; and
Eli with Archbishop Harry
Flynn.*

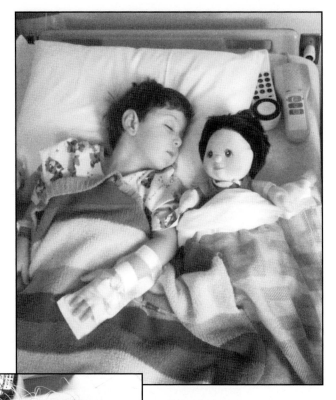

*Eli has had more than his share of medical tests and surgeries.* **Above:** *Eli rests prior to testing at Tulane University Medical Center in New Orleans.* **Left:** *He's wired up for the test, an electroencephalogram (EEG), to determine if he had irregular neurological activity, which can be the cause of seizures.*

*Several mothers who read* Waiting for Eli *were influenced by its pro-life message and made the decision to reject abortion and bring their babies to term, despite the knowledge that the babies would be born with birth defects.* **Above:** *Tracey Hargrave with husband Jason and son Michael.* **Below:** *Camryn Hayes and Kyle Carmello.*

*Messages of hope and encouragement in the book,* Waiting for Eli, *have been well received by people from all walks of life.*
**Above:** *Danielle Leger with her visually impaired daughter, Nadia.*
**Left:** *Samantha LaHaye with her newly adopted special-needs child, Aubrey.*

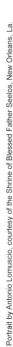

*Blessed Father Francis Xavier Seelos, who is in line for canonization to sainthood by the Catholic Church, was a missionary priest who served the seriously ill and dying in a yellow fever epidemic in New Orleans in the mid-1860s. We prayed regularly for his intercession in the cause of Eli's health and well-being.*

watch cartoons with Ephraim. When I put Eli down on the floor, he began to cry. I stepped back to look at him, and he appeared to be in the same state he was in earlier in the week when Ashley had to take him to the hospital in New Orleans.

Ashley was at work, so I called my mother-in-law, who, like Ashley, is a Registered Nurse. I described Eli's condition. In short order, she came over to get the boys and take them to her house to dye Easter eggs. She told me she would call if she saw that anything seemed to be wrong with Eli.

An hour later, my phone rang. Something was wrong with Eli.

I hung up the phone, got into my car immediately and drove quickly to the emergency room at Women's & Children's Hospital. Ashley and her mom were there with the boys. The second I saw Eli, I knew we were going back to the hospital in New Orleans. My mom came and picked up Ephraim about the same time Eli and Ashley were boarding the ambulance for the trip to New Orleans.

I was both shocked and scared. I remembered those terrible feelings of helplessness and uncertainty when we first found out about Eli's condition. I was re-entering the realm of the unknown, and again I could feel that the only thing that would carry our family through this was the power of prayer.

On my way home to pack a bag for Ashley and one for me, I called a friend who was leading a group of students from our school on a mission trip to Puerto Rico. I know I must have sounded frantic and desperate as I told him what was happening. I asked him to pray for us, and he promised that he and his students would do so every day while they were on the mission trip.

After packing our bags, I headed for my in-laws' house to meet up with Randy and Ann. I was to ride with Ann while Randy would follow in my car. When I got to their house, Randy rushed up to me while I was still in my car.

"We've got to go," he said emphatically. "Ann, stay calm and please drive carefully."

As we sped down the road toward the interstate, Ann told me Ashley had called earlier and said that Eli had a seizure in the ambulance; it happened right outside of Baton Rouge, and they were stopping at a hospital near I-10 to get emergency help to stabilize him.

I began to despair. Eli had defied all the medical odds stacked against him. He was a beautiful and vibrant child who was intellectually and emotionally at the same level as any other two-year-old. Despite his physical limitations, I knew that if his mind worked well he could do nearly anything he wanted in life. Was that prospect now slipping away? While these thoughts were crossing my mind, my mother-in-law was very upset and was fighting back tears.

"It's not in our control. All we can do is pray,"

she said.

And that is exactly what we did, the whole way to New Orleans. We prayed the rosary for the entire trip.

Meanwhile, Eli was admitted to the Pediatric Intensive Care Unit (PICU) on the sixth floor of Tulane Medical Center. Ann, Randy and I arrived an hour or so later. Soon after that, Ashley and I met with Eli's neurosurgeon. Dr. John Walsh had been Eli's surgeon since his birth and was familiar with all of his medical needs. Approaching 75 years of age, he had been practicing his profession for more than 40 years. Eli's pediatrician, my uncle, had recommended him.

Dr. Walsh informed us that Eli would have emergency surgery that evening. He said the MRI showed that a cyst that he had been aware of in Eli's brain had grown over the past six to eight months and was applying pressure to the ventricles in his brain, thus preventing the shunt from draining the spinal fluid from the ventricles. The operation was intended to restore proper flow of the fluid from the brain to the spinal cord.

As the doctor walked away to prepare his team for surgery, I thought back to the afternoon the day before when I was watching my sons play in the pool – quite a different scene from the nightmare we were now living.

It was ten o'clock on Holy Saturday night, and

the third floor of the hospital where surgeries take place was deserted except for Ashley and me and her parents. The four of us sat there together praying and waiting. There is a flat screen overlooking the waiting room desk and the phone sitting on it. Under normal circumstances, the screen displays a list of all patients having surgery, and their loved ones are called to the phone to get updates from the doctors who are performing the surgeries. On this night, only one entry was showing on the screen: Eli Judice – In Surgery – Dr. Walsh.

As we sat there physically and emotionally drained, praying gave me a sense of peace and strength that certainly went beyond my understanding. I had felt that way only once before – when we were waiting for Eli to be born.

At two o'clock in the morning, Dr. Walsh appeared in the doorway of the waiting room then walked calmly toward us.

"I believe we had a successful surgery. I was able to insert a draining tube into the cyst. I believe over time the cyst will begin to collapse and that will alleviate the pressure on the brain. This will allow the fluid to flow normally," Dr. Walsh said.

Ashley was able to be with Eli in the PICU after he left the recovery room following surgery. Ashley and I slept four or five hours in a room made available for parents of children in the PICU. Ann and Randy went to a separate sleeping area.

Waking up at Tulane Hospital on Easter morning was not the way I had envisioned the weekend playing out. I understood Eli would be in the hospital for at least a week and possibly longer if there were complications from the surgery.

Knowing St. Joseph's Catholic Church was within walking distance of the hospital, and after getting to see Eli for a short time in the morning, Ashley and I were comfortable with our leaving to attend Mass. She knew her mother and father would be at Eli's bedside and would contact us immediately if there was a problem of any kind. Eli still had not regained consciousness since receiving anesthesia prior to the operation.

While attending Mass, I realized that once again Eli's life had brought a lot of people in a lot of places to prayer. It was a mildly consoling thought, given the circumstances.

The priest was in the midst of his homily when Ashley got a text message from her mom. She walked outside to call her back. Half-listening to the priest, I sat anxiously waiting to hear what Ashley had been told. She returned to our pew and said in a very calm but exhausted tone of voice:

"He needs another surgery. They are starting at noon."

Looking at my watch, I could see that we would not be able to stay for the whole Mass. We did receive communion then bolted out of the church. We found ourselves jogging back toward the hospital. The streets were empty, and I felt like I was in the Twilight Zone. I called my parents in mid-stride and asked them to get our large extended family together for a rosary. They said they would.

Out of breath, we reached the hospital and got to see Eli for a few moments as he was being prepared for surgery. Helpless, apprehensive and teary-eyed, we prayed that the Lord would be with Eli and with his surgeon.

# Chapter 16

## *An Easter miracle*

Easter Sunday at noon Eli was rolled back into the operating room for a second surgery in less than eight hours.

Like last time, Ashley and I and her parents sat together in the waiting room praying the rosary. While the lengthy operation was under way, I received two very welcome phone calls, one from my mom, who asked for an update on Eli's condition so she could share it with our extended family, and the other from a friend who has a child with *spina bifida*.

Four hours after the surgery began, Dr. Walsh came to see us in the waiting room. Looking very tired, he slowly pulled down his surgery mask and gave us a little half-smile.

"I believe the operation was a complete success.

Everything seems to be draining properly, and by the time you get back up to the sixth floor your son should be in the PICU and you can see him," he said.

Ashley and I thanked him and made our way back upstairs to see Eli before we began winding down for the evening. We were physically and emotionally spent. Same for Ashley's parents.

A few hours later, we received a disheartening call from the intern who was working with Dr. Walsh. He said he had viewed the MRI following surgery and was almost positive Eli would require additional surgery the following morning.

We could hardly believe what we were hearing, but we were resolved to continue praying.

Now, when we were in New Orleans for Eli's birth a little more than two years earlier, I visited the Shrine of Blessed Father Francis Xavier Seelos, a holy man who is being considered for canonization to sainthood by the Catholic Church. He was a nineteenth century missionary priest who came to New Orleans to minister to gravely ill people stricken in a yellow fever epidemic. After a year in the semi-tropical climate of southern Louisiana, he too contracted the disease and died from it. Following his death, a number of miraculous healings were attributed to his intercessory prayers.

Since my visit to his shrine, I had been praying for his intercession on Eli's behalf. I'd been using a special petition that concludes with these words: "Through his (Fr. Seelos') prayers, please grant me this favor."

Again, I prayed this prayer at Eli's bedside. I stood there looking at my son, so small, so helpless. He lay there nearly motionless, still unconscious from the anesthesia, hooked up to life-supporting machines and monitors of various kinds. All of his hair had been shaved off for the second surgery.

I fought back tears as I prayed in silence, seeking the supernatural assistance of Fr. Seelos. I asked that, through Fr. Seelos' intercession, Jesus would heal Eli's cyst and cure the medical condition that was threatening his life. Then I prayed the rosary, asking Mary, the mother of Jesus, to help my ailing son.

When I finished, it was after 10 p.m., and I was so tired that I could no longer stand up. I slept most of that night out of sheer exhaustion. But despite the severity of the situation, I felt at peace, believing that everything was going to be okay.

I didn't realize it at the time, but my mom and dad had been gathering a small army of prayer warriors back home to join us in prayer. Mom had sent out an e-mail to our extended family and friends – all people of faith. She wrote:

*The battle is not over. Eli urgently needs your prayers now more than ever before. After two brain surgeries in less than 24 hours, the problem with the*

cyst in his head is causing a very gifted neurosurgeon,
his parents and his grandparents much anguish and
heartache. Many of our family and extended family
came to our home and said a rosary for Eli today,
giving up a portion of their holiday.... We will always
be grateful for your support.

However, we learned earlier this evening that the
latest scan shows the problem is still not solved, and
Eli faces the possibility of a third surgery tomorrow.

How much can this poor child endure?

We have a strong faith and continue to believe
prayer is the ultimate answer to this problem. What
doctors are sometimes unable to do, God sometimes
does. All we have to do is pray and believe. It is our
faith that has sustained us and kept us focused.

The next morning, Ashley and I went into the
PICU to see Eli and to meet with Dr. Walsh. We saw
that Eli was breathing easily, lying flat on his back,
uncovered, with his diaper on.

Ashley kissed him and stood on the side of his
bed holding his right hand. I kissed him and stood
on the other side of the bed holding his left hand.
I felt a light tap on my shoulder. It was Dr. Walsh.

"Is he responding to your touch?" he asked.

"Yes," I replied.

"Please come with me," he said.

He led us into a small room next to the nursing
station and closed the door behind us. His resident,

an Asian man who seemed to be with him all the time, sat across from us with a baffled look on his face. Dr. Walsh, too, seemed perplexed about something, though not in a way that concerned me.

But what the doctor had to say really got our attention.

"Eli's cyst was preventing the tubing of the shunt from draining properly and was thus causing the initial problem. This procedure is quite normal in children with the type of *spina bifida* Eli has, and I have dealt with it in numerous similar situations.

"The operation is so technical that I often have to navigate draining tubes around the hard outer membrane of the cyst to allow the fluid to drain from the ventricles into the spinal cord.

"In the initial operation late Saturday night, I was hopeful that the cyst would decrease in size over an extended period of time, thus collapsing and freeing up the ventricles and allowing the shunt to function properly. Since that was unsuccessful, we went back in.

"During the second operation last night, I and my team believed we had navigated the tubing around the hard outer membrane of the cyst and that the fluid was draining properly. It appeared to be doing so, based on what I observed on the monitor. I watched it for quite a while to make sure.

"The CT scan taken after surgery last night showed the tubing had not actually reached the ventricles, as previously believed, but instead fell off into the cyst, draining it at a rate that caused it to decrease in size by 75 percent overnight.

"Either your son had a malformed ventricle that is now draining properly with the aid of a shunt, or it is the first time in my career when operating on patients with this condition that I have encountered a cyst like this with no outer membrane.

"I suspected that Eli's ventricles would continue to enlarge due to increased pressure on the brain because of the cyst, even after the first surgery. However, even after the two consecutive surgeries, since Eli has been here, the MRI's have consistently shown that his ventricles have never enlarged. There is a possibility that after the cyst collapses and eventually dissolves, he may no longer need a shunt. What I am seeing in the MRI now would not warrant a need for one.

"I am planning on writing a medical study on this, because in 40 years of practicing this type of medicine I have never seen a case like this."

Gripping my rosary in my right hand and feeling my wife's hand slide into mine, I watched Ashley as she responded to the doctor.

"Never seen a case like this before?"

Shaking her head from side to side, she continued:

"My husband has been praying for over a year that Eli's cyst would be healed and that he would no longer need a shunt."

Dr. Walsh, who usually talked directly to Ashley because of her knowledge of medicine, turned his head and spoke to me.

"I am going to leave Eli alone where he is and monitor him. He does not need another surgery. I hope that very soon we can get you all home and you can return to the normalcy of your lives," he said.

I walked out of the PICU into the waiting room. My mother-in-law stood up from her chair with rosary in hand and my father-in-law stood beside her.

"What did he say?" she asked.

"Are you ready for this? The cyst shrunk 75 percent overnight, and he doesn't need surgery!" I replied.

"Praise Jesus!" she added.

My voice began to crack and tears squirted from my eyes.

"It's a miracle," I said.

My father-in-law and I embraced; both of us were crying. I could see out of the corner of my eye that my wife and her mother were hugging and crying as well.

# Chapter 17

## *A return to the Shrine of Blessed Father Seelos*

The Monday after Easter, I breathed a big sigh of relief, knowing Eli was not going to have to endure a third surgery. It did my heart good to see him sitting up in bed for short periods of time and watching his favorite show on a portable DVD player.

The next day, we were visited by our friend, Fr. Manny Fernandez. He's the healing priest who, while Ashley was pregnant with Eli, had been instrumental in providing both spiritual and psychological healing for Ashley and me. He came to the hospital at my request, and his presence was quite a comfort to us. He visited with us near Eli's bedside for about 45 minutes, then he prayed over the three of us.

Several times in the past, I'd told myself that on my next visit to New Orleans I'd return to the

Shrine of Blessed Father Seelos. I was confident that praying there brought and would continue to bring many spiritual benefits. Also, I wanted to visit again in gratitude for Fr. Seelos' intercession for the health of my son.

I firmly believe that Fr. Seelos was instrumental in Eli's miraculous healing on Easter Sunday. I believe the sudden reduction of the size of the life-threatening cyst in Eli's brain was truly a miracle, not explainable by any natural or medical law. It was a supernatural occurrence, brought about by God Himself, and manifested in a physical way.

On Wednesday morning, my father-in-law, Randy, and I went to the shrine, a 20-minute drive from the hospital. We met the director, Fr. Byron Miller. Turns out, he knew who we were because he had read my book and was intrigued by what I had written about my first visit to the shrine.

We went up a set of stairs to his office on the second floor. I sat across from him and explained what had happened over the Easter weekend, starting with the time I prayed for Fr. Seelos' intercession at Eli's bedside. Fr. Miller was very attentive and commented on how pleased he was about the fact that the shrine had been a place of comfort and healing for me the last time I visited. He said he hoped the visit this time would provide similar benefits.

He gave me a card with his e-mail address and asked me to send him Eli's room number, promising he would be by to see Eli and to give him a special blessing.

Fr. Miller then led us to the shrine and escorted us through the door. We were the only people there. I sat down next to the life-size bronze statue of Fr. Seelos. The statue literally sits on a bench, and its arm extends over the back of the bench. Visitors are invited to sit there, next to the statue, and to pray. So I sat for five minutes, praying and thanking the spirit of Fr. Seelos for his intercession on behalf of my son.

Then I accompanied Randy to a nearby room containing a glass-encased area where Fr. Seelos' mortal remains are buried. We knelt together in front of it and prayed. As we were about to leave, I thanked Randy for coming with me to the shrine and for everything he and Ann had done on Eli's behalf. He responded, "No, Bud, thank you."

I've had a few special moments like this with Randy, and they have all been because of our mutual interest in Eli. For me, one of the greatest blessings from all of the struggles with Eli and his fragile health has been the forming of a bond with my in-laws.

When we returned to the hospital, I e-mailed Fr. Miller with Eli's room number, and around 3 p.m. he came for a visit. After chatting for a while, Fr. Miller proceeded to bless Eli; he touched Eli's forehead with the cross that Fr. Seelos carried with him during his ministry to the sick, then recited a prayer for Eli's continued recovery.

Right about this time, Dr. Walsh knocked on the door and entered the room. He said he'd ordered a CT scan for Eli and that depending on the results he'd be able to tell us when Eli could go home.

He discharged Eli the next morning and asked us to bring him back in a few weeks for a check-up and to remove the sutures from the incision spot on Eli's head.

A month later, Dr Walsh examined Eli and told Ashley all was well and that he didn't need to see Eli again for a year.

In short order, things returned to normal at our house, and Eli was accepted into a pre-kindergarten program at the same school his brother attends. The school authorities observed what Ashley and I have known for a while: Eli is a pretty smart kid. His cognitive ability is strong, and tests show he is functioning intellectually at a high level for his age. His diction is very good and his comprehension of words and phrases is excellent for such a little guy.

You never know, he might turn out to be a genius. But his mother and I will be satisfied as long as he continues to be a happy, healthy child.

## Chapter 18

# *A breath away from Heaven*

Tired and run down after a hectic week, I walked through the front door of my house on a Friday afternoon in early February 2012. I was looking forward to a restful weekend. The past week had been a whirlwind, as each night I attended some function, mostly in connection with extracurricular activities at my school.

The previous night, Ashley and I had the pleasure of meeting Archbishop Harry Flynn, who was in town for a fundraising event for a new Catholic school called John Paul II Academy. The Archbishop was to be the keynote speaker. Now retired, he had been the Archbishop of the Archdiocese of Minneapolis-St. Paul for a number of years and earlier, from 1986 to 1994, served as Bishop of the Diocese of Lafayette. He was and is a strong leader in the Catholic Church and is known as a top-flight orator and homilist. We could hardly wait to hear his talk.

So, it was Friday evening and Ashley and I were getting ready for the fundraising event. Eli and Ephraim were playing on the floor in front of the TV. Ashley's dad, Randy, who would be babysitting that night, was sitting in the rocking chair in the TV room. Ashley was in our bedroom putting some final touches on her hair and makeup. Also in the bedroom were Ashley's mom, Ann, and one of Ashley's aunts, Marcelle Kokenge, who would be coming with us to the gala. I was pacing in the den and checking my watch every now and then — well, actually, every minute or two. We were running late, and I was getting nervous.

I noticed Eli seemed a bit groggy. He was fighting a sinus drip, which is very common for any child in south Louisiana at this time of year. After a little sing-along with the television and dancing, that included moving his head back and forth and waving his arms in the air, he stopped on a dime and looked like he was frozen. Thinking that was odd, I called out to him.

"Eli, are you okay?"

In a flash, Randy was down on his knees beside me and Eli. We both were speaking directly to Eli, but he was staring into space. He appeared to be gagging and trying to clear his airway as though something was blocking it. Randy attempted a finger sweep through his mouth to see if something was lodged in there. I watched intently as his mouth began to move in a chewing motion and his face and lips were turning blue.

Then he went completely limp and fell into Randy's arms.

Randy began running down the hallway carrying Eli and yelling in a calm but assertive voice, "Ann! Ann!" I sat there a moment frozen in time in a state of shock. Ephraim was standing behind me, and he too was frozen, not knowing what to do or say. Quickly regaining my senses, I ran behind Randy in the hallway. Then I heard Ashley and Ann repeatedly saying, "Eli! Eli! Eli!"

Both Ashley and Ann are Registered Nurses who encounter situations similar to this one at work on a daily basis. However, administering emergency medical care to a patient and doing so for someone in your immediate family are two different things.

When I got to the doorway of our room, Ashley was holding Eli upright and administering back blows to try to force a foreign object from his throat, in case something was stuck there. It was one of the most sobering moments of my life. Laying Eli on his back, Ashley and Ann both said in a panicked voice:

"Call an ambulance!"

I quickly dialed 911 and began giving information to the emergency responder on the other end. As I tried to focus on delivering the necessary information I could hear Ashley and Ann administering CPR.

"Come on, breathe!" Ashley was saying with desperation in her voice.

The only other thing I could hear was her aunt praying the Hail Mary. I tried to join in the prayer while speaking into the phone.

By the time I hung up Eli was lying on his side and crying.

He was breathing! Thank God!

Then it hit me that Ephraim was all alone in the den, so I darted down the hall. Just as I caught sight of him, I also saw the ambulance and fire truck pulling up into our yard.

The Emergency Medical Technicians and the firemen entered the house simultaneously and seemed almost shocked as Ashley walked into the den holding Eli. I think they were expecting an adult.

Ephraim was frozen in the position he had been in a few moments earlier. I knelt down, took hold of his arms and looked into his eyes. I saw the same fear I was feeling in the pit of my stomach. I talked to him in a calm and reassuring voice.

"He is going to be okay. Ephraim, look at me. Eli is going to be okay."

For a moment he appeared to be processing what I was saying, then I saw the fear return and he began to cry.

"Ephraim, Eli is going to be okay," I repeated, trying to convince myself as much as Ephraim.

With the look of concern only a loving big brother could have, and with a whimper, he asked:

"Is Eli going to be okay?"

Fighting back tears, I nodded my head. I could see a sense of peace coming over him as I wiped away his tears. He seemed to be okay.

I redirected my eyes to Ashely as she called my name.

"When I know what's going on I'll call you from the hospital. I love you," she said as she walked out the door following the paramedics, who were rolling Eli out on a gurney.

As they drove away, I called my parents, and my dad said they'd be over right away.

Next, I called my friends Dewey and Nikki Thevis, who were waiting for Ashley and me to join them at the gala. They're the ones who invited us, and they're good friends with Archbishop Flynn. I reached Nikki and told her something terrible had happened to Eli and that he was being rushed to the hospital in an ambulance, and that we wouldn't be able to make it to the event. I gave her a few of the details, and she expressed her deepest sympathy and concern for all of us.

"We'll be praying for y'all," she said in a warm and reassuring voice. "Please keep me posted."

"I will," I responded, fighting back tears.

# Chapter 19

## *A prayer for Eli*

I paced back and forth between my bedroom and the living room while Randy sat in the den watching television. Both of us were trying to occupy our anxious minds while waiting to hear something from Ashley about Eli's condition. It had been an hour since they left in the ambulance.

Ephraim, too, was very unsettled over what he had witnessed. He continually inquired about his brother.

"Dad, is Eli going to have surgery again? He must have something wrong with his brain," he said.

He must have repeated that 20 times in that first hour.

Seeing that I was having trouble gathering my thoughts for what lay ahead, my parents, who had arrived shortly after the ambulance left, decided to take Ephraim elsewhere to get his mind off what he just witnessed and to allow me to prepare myself for the phone call I knew would be coming.

After eating a little something, out of necessity rather than hunger, I was sitting on the couch in the den praying silently when the phone rang. After a brief conversation with Ashley, I knew it was going to be a very long night and potentially a long stay at Tulane Medical Center in New Orleans. She told me the radiologist who read the CT scan said it appeared one of the ventricles in Eli's brain was enlarged, suggesting there could be another shunt malfunction. So, another surgery seemed imminent.

Ashley and Eli would be transported immediately to the hospital in New Orleans by ambulance. Ashley's parents and I were going to be coming in right behind them. This whole episode seemed to be playing out the same way it had the last time, less than a year earlier, when Eli was rushed to New Orleans for surgery to correct a shunt malfunction.

As the ambulance with Eli and Ashley left Women's & Children's Hospital in Lafayette and began its eastward journey on I-10 toward New Orleans, Ashley prayed that God would spare our son. Eli lay on a portable bed with an IV taped to his left arm and hand. He looked so small and vulnerable and innocent. Ashley sat next to him, holding his right hand, praying, hoping, studying his beautiful face. A paramedic sat nearby, observing mother and child.

Tired and weak from the ordeal, Eli fell asleep soon after the ambulance got on the road. When he woke from time to time, Ashley would hold his hand and speak softly to him with words of reassurance. She would nuzzle up to his face and kiss him on his cheeks and on his nose and on his eyebrows. When he was asleep, she prayed the rosary in silence.

The ambulance was already en route to New Orleans when I began packing my bags and Ann began doing the same for Ashley. Then we left our house to go over to Ann and Randy's so they could pack. The three of us would ride together to New Orleans. My parents had agreed to care for Ephraim while we were gone.

We left Lafayette around 8:15 p.m. When we got on the highway, my thoughts went back to the man of prayer we were supposed to be listening to that evening, Archbishop Harry Flynn. As we headed east on U.S. Hwy. 90 toward New Orleans, I was praying, and I felt the same peace and reassurance I had the night before when we had been in the archbishop's company. I was confident that once he heard about what had happened to Eli he would be praying for all of us. With this thought in my mind, I felt at peace, and the fear that had such a grip on me earlier lost its power and disappeared into the night.

About the same time we were getting on the road, Archbishop Flynn was being introduced by master of ceremonies Raymond Arroyo of EWTN fame. The archbishop stood at the podium and addressed the crowd of some 500 people who were gathered in a large ballroom of the Cajundome Convention Center.

"Before I begin, there is a gentleman who was going to be here tonight, a teacher at St. Thomas More High School, Chad Judice. He wrote that wonderful book, *Waiting for Eli*. His wife and he brought a child to life who they knew would not be well. Chad and Ashley were going to be here tonight, but their child had a seizure, and they are on their way to New Orleans, where there will be some surgery in the morning. So, I would ask that together we put this child under the mantle of Our Lady and ask her to take care of this beautiful child, this sign of life – and give the parents the courage they need to face whatever is the will of God."

And with this, Archbishop Flynn began to pray in a strong voice, and the crowd joined in, in what seemed like a single voice, and the prayer of petition for the intercession of Mary, the mother of Christ the Lord, rose up and filled the room.

> *Hail Mary, full of grace, the Lord is with thee. Blessed art thou among women and blessed is the fruit of thy womb, Jesus. Holy Mary, mother of God, pray for us sinners now and at the hour of our death. Amen.*

"And, Our Lady, protect Eli. Jesus, be with him

tonight, tomorrow and always. Amen," Archbishop Flynn concluded.

As the event in Lafayette was ending, the ambulance arrived at Tulane Medical Center in New Orleans. Ashley signed papers to admit Eli to the hospital, then carried our sleepy boy to their room.

While Ashley and Eli were settling down in the room, Ann, Randy and I were still en route to New Orleans.

It was a very long drive. What should have taken three hours took nearly five. The bridge over the Mississippi River we would ordinarily take when we got close to New Orleans was closed. So, we had to take a detour, which cost us a lot of time.

While on the road, we got a call from Ashley saying they had reached the hospital and were now in a room. Eli had no complications on the way over and was sleeping peacefully.

By the time we finally arrived it was after 1 a.m. We were all exhausted, to put it mildly. We resolved to get as much rest as possible, considering Eli was facing major surgery and a long recovery period ahead.

Waking up early the following morning, I heard Eli's sweet voice.

"Mommy, can I have some juice?"

Eli appeared to be fine, as though what happened the night before was just a bad dream.

After having some coffee and a light breakfast, we

resumed our anxious wait.

Some of the hospital's residents had come to make rounds and examined Eli, but Ashley was adamant that we speak with Dr. Walsh, Eli's doctor, after he examined the CT scan. Twice in the past radiologists in Lafayette had misread the CT scans. So in order to get a clear diagnosis of what was happening with Eli we wanted to hear it directly from the doctor who'd been with him since birth.

It was mid-morning when Dr. Walsh walked into the room and delivered the good though shocking news. He told us that the ventricle in Eli's brain was not enlarged and that his shunt was working well. There had been no change since Eli was here in April of 2011, at Eastertime, 10 months earlier. The angle of the scan may have caused the person who read it to suspect a shunt malfunction. We learned, however, it was not uncommon for a child with a shunt to have irregular neurological activity while extremely tired or fighting a common cold; these things can trigger a seizure.

Dr. Walsh ordered an EEG and put Eli on anti-seizure medication, to be taken twice a day. This is prescribed for many people who suffer with epilepsy. The doctor recommended that we have a pediatric neurologist read the EEG results back in Lafayette and monitor the dosage prescribed. Although he was ready to discharge us, Ashley wanted to stay one more night to monitor Eli's reaction to the medication.

Learning of yet another condition that could be a problem for Eli was sobering for both Ashley and me. The blessing in connection with this was knowing what caused the seizure and knowing there was something we could do to reduce the chances of it happening again.

We left the hospital in New Orleans early Sunday afternoon, much relieved and ready to go home. It was a bright, sunshiny day. Eli rode in his carseat in the middle in the back, with his mother on one side and his grandmother on the other. I drove and Randy sat in the front. Eli entertained himself with a kid's movie on a DVD player, dozing off from time to time. Ashley held Eli's hand, watched a little of the movie with him, and chatted with her mother.

Eli seemed as happy and content as he could be – done with the hospital, headed home to his own bed, a good movie on the screen, juice and snacks readily at hand, mom to the left of him and grandma to the right, dad and grandpa nearby. For this little guy, all was right with the world.

# Afterword

## *A day with Eli*

My head pops off the pillow and I quickly turn to check the clock on the nightstand. It is sometime between 6 and 7 a.m. I haven't slept later than this for as long as I can remember.

The Saturday morning routine plays itself out pretty much the same way it has for the past three years. The same questions flood my mind at this time of the morning: *Is that Eli I hear calling my name in the other room? What time was it last night when he was last catheterized?*

I'll take the same steps this morning to give Eli his medications before attempting to feed him breakfast. I'll take the pill capsule apart and drop the powder into a spoon with a small portion of vanilla or chocolate ice cream. I'll drop the second pill into a medicine bottle cap and fill it with water. Using a syringe,

I'll draw anti-seizure medication from a small bottle, then coax Eli into swallowing it.

Soon, Eli will be on his mat on the living room floor watching his favorite TV show, "The Fresh Beat Band."

And then there is Eli's brother, Ephraim, who will want his chocolate milk and Honey Bun when he comes walking into the scene half-awake and with his hair sticking up in the back.

This whole Saturday morning routine plays itself out in my mind before it actually happens, before my feet hit the floor in my bedroom. Whether it's the weekdays with Ashley in charge or me on the weekend, it's the same play, just directed by a different parent.

Summertime is much less hectic because we are not trying to get Ephraim ready for school and me ready for work. From August through the following May, the daily routine has more firm deadlines than the summer.

I guess that is why by the end of the school year both Ashley and I are ready to drop. We're searching for some downtime, although at times that seems like a distant memory of something that may never be again. We both have full-time jobs in the working world, but for most of the year we are working outside of our respective day jobs as well. Rearing any child properly is a full-time job – Just ask anyone who has done it! – but adding a child with special needs into the mix is something completely different.

Ashley has worked every weekend since the spring of 2009. Fortunately, our parents live in the same town as we do and help us with the kids on a regular basis. I have said many prayers of thanksgiving for their commitment to us and our special circumstances. They have taught us a lot about the nature of love and sacrifice. These qualities have been embraced by our entire family, including Ephraim.

Because of Eli's special needs, Ephraim has willingly given up more than his fair share of attention and routine kids' activities. For instance, each time Ephraim attends a birthday party for a friend he must avoid contact with items that contain latex, such as balloons. Latex allergies are common among children with Eli's condition, and the best way to prevent the allergy is to completely avoid latex – or anyone who has been in contact with it. This chemical is present in many everyday items, especially in small children's toys. Ephraim never complains and has come to accept at a young age that life is not always about getting what he wants.

Ephraim inspires me to be a more selfless father and husband every day.

Ashley, too, is truly amazing. Her level of commitment to getting Eli what he needs is matched only by her commitment to her patients in the Neonatal Intensive Care Unit at Women's & Children's Hospital. There is something to be done for Eli every few hours of the day, and if Ashley was not already a Registered Nurse, she practically could have become one by learning to care for Eli.

Every morning the first thing Eli needs is his urinary catheterization. This process is repeated every three hours at least five times a day, depending on the amount of his recent fluid intake. Because of the nerve damage to his spinal cord, he needs catheterization to empty his bladder completely. Without this treatment, the urine that would remain would begin to produce unhealthy forms of bacteria that can cause a urinary tract infection. These UTI's are very common in individuals with *spina bifida*. Eli developed his first UTI in the summer of 2010 and has had only one other bout with it since.

Since we began catheterizing, Eli is required to take two different types of medication by mouth. The first, Detrol, is used to stop his continuous bladder spasms, which if left unchecked would make it difficult to empty his bladder completely. A complication from this would be kidney reflux that eventually could cause permanent kidney damage. The second medication, Macrodantin, is used to prevent urinary tract infections.

We have to wait about an hour or so before feeding Eli breakfast because the medications typically suppress his appetite. Until April of 2011, when he had his last major surgery, he had not weighed more than 20 pounds. But since then his appetite has improved.

However, lately he has been more interested in playing with his food than eating it – which is so typical of a three-year-old.

For a child his age, Eli has had a lot of therapy, ranging from physical and occupational therapy to speech therapy. His physical therapy involves skills that will improve his upper body strength and eventually give him as much mobility below the waist as possible. He has made great strides in this area. He has improved his core strength in his abdomen – which gives him more independence getting in and out of his wheelchair – and he is now walking short distances. With the aid of a walker and a specialized device that supports his entire body and aids in the stepping process, Eli continues to exceed the physical limitations the doctors predicted. He has a scheduled physical therapy session once a week, and we continue these activities two or three times a week on our own when he is not in therapy.

Occupational therapy is designed to help Eli develop motor skills that will improve his quality of life and hopefully provide him with some independence. They consist of things like feeding himself, tying his shoes, writing his name, and dressing himself. For the first two years of Eli's life, an occupational therapist visited our home to work with him through a service offered by the State of Louisiana. His therapist continually commented that he was doing things cognitively that other children with similar disabilities were unable to do. It became apparent very early on that although he has physical limitations, his intellectual state not only surpasses what was expected but functions at a very high level. I'm happy to report that in August of 2012 he began pre-kindergarten classes at St. Pius Elementary School.

Eli's speech therapist made a monthly visit to our home for the first year of Eli's life. This initial push to develop his speech has paid off tremendously. He speaks very fluently for his age and can carry on a continual conversation with adults.

His mind is a mystery to us. His older brother didn't do some of the things Eli is doing now when he was Eli's age. I believe that when children are lacking in some of their capabilities, nature helps them to overcompensate in other areas.

When Eli flashes that golden smile and inquisitive look, one has to recognize that all the wheels are turning in his mental engine. It is exciting and fulfilling to watch it unfold. But it's the moments when he says simple things like "Daddy, I love you" that really floor me.

Eli's favorite piece of equipment is his "stander." It allows him to stand erect for a period of time, bringing constant blood flow to his lower extremities while keeping his femur bone in line with his hip socket. His left leg below his knee is turned slightly inward, and his standing along with other therapy may help to eventually straighten it out. Because Eli does not have the leg strength to hold himself up, his stander provides him with that capability. Although we were hopeful that the bone would straighten through this process, doctors have indicated that Eli will need surgery to correct this.

The stander looks like a Roman chariot and gives Eli the ability to be mobile at home without being confined to his wheelchair. He uses the wheelchair in public when we have to move him over a good distance in a short period of time. As he grows older and wants to keep up with his friends, he'll use his wheelchair more.

Eli has seen more doctors in three years than I have in my entire life. His neurosurgeon monitors his shunt that regulates his hydrocephalus, and a neurologist monitors the irregular activity in his brain since his seizure in February of 2012. He had a cardiologist for a while, until his post-birth heart condition corrected itself. Now and for years to come a urologist will help him deal with issues of incontinence. Eli's orthopedic doctor monitors his unaligned hips and bone structure and continues to give advice on how to best strengthen his lower extremities.

Finally, a pediatrician will continue to oversee and care for him when he contracts common childhood illnesses such as the common cold.

This is certainly not the life I foresaw my family having ten years ago, but we have accepted and embraced it. God's plan is much broader than we possibly could have imagined, and His reach through Eli has proven to be immeasurable.

Doctors told us Eli would never walk, yet he walks today with the assistance of his equipment. Regardless of where the road leads our family in the future, I know that God will light the way as we continue our walk with Eli.

# Appendix

## *Letters of support for Eli's story*

*Of the many endorsements and letters of support for* Waiting for Eli, *none has been more poignant than those coming from men of the cloth from various parts of the United States. Following are three of those letters, one referring to the book as "a profound testimony to the Gospel of Life."*

---

In *Waiting for Eli*, Chad Judice chronicles his spiritual journey from fear of one's personal limitations to self-abandonment to the divine mercy of God's providence. The story of his spiritual progression, as he prepares for the birth of his son, Eli, functions as a profound testimony to the Gospel of Life and to the underlying truth that faith is perfected through trial and suffering.

The author takes the universal pro-life message of the sanctity of human life and uses it to illustrate how the life of one child can sanctify the lives of the community of believers who witness to the power of prayer.

It is always a singular grace when God inspires us to be courageous and hopeful through the lives and sacrifices of others who persevere, especially one as young as Eli Judice.

*–Daniel Cardinal DiNardo*
Archbishop of Galveston-Houston
Chair of the Committee for Pro-Life Activities
U.S. Conference of Catholic Bishops

\* \* \*

The world judges the value of human life by physical perfection, but God sees things differently. To Him, we are perfectly loveable in our imperfection. Uplifting in its reverence for human life in its most fragile stages, *Waiting for Eli* will encourage pro-life activists everywhere, from the most seasoned to the newly initiated.

*–Father Frank Pavone*
Priests for Life

\* \* \*

Dear Chad,

I just finished reading your book, and I thank you for sharing this story to remind us all what it means to "walk by faith and not by sight."

This is one of the most inspiring stories I have ever read.

Most people probably do not know what kind of courage and faith is required to make this journey, which is ongoing, and then to write about it, speak about it and live it each day.

You and your family are teaching us all some of the most valuable lessons on faith that can be learned. These are the lessons that cannot be conveyed by a textbook. They must be lived, embraced and shared in the humility that comes from constant prayer and copious tears.

Needless to say, I enjoyed the book very much and thank God that He has given you and your young family the grace to be a light to the nations.

I thank God for surrounding you with people like Fr. Joe Breaux, John Listi, Lance Strother and so many others at St. Thomas More. You could not ask for a better support team! These guys are just amazing, and I know that God put them in your life to be with you during this time of testing and striving. I am sure that you know that these are not fair-weather friends but are indeed the kind that every man needs and longs for.

The course of events that you have chronicled in your book with the providential meetings of people, places and events is just astounding. As St. John Vianney used to say, "The good God is so good!"

Peace and Blessings,

*-Fr. Matthew P. Higginbotham*
Pastor, Immaculate Heart of Mary Church
Crowley, La.

# *Index*

Note: Page numbers in *italics* refer to photographs or maps.

# *About the Author...*

CHAD JUDICE is a high school teacher of civics and American history at St. Thomas More Catholic High School in Lafayette, Louisiana. He began teaching there in 2005 after teaching and coaching basketball the previous four years at Cathedral-Carmel, another Catholic school in Lafayette.

He is the winner of the 2010 Lafayette Education Foundation Teacher of the Year Award in the Inspirational Teacher category.

An active public speaker, he is the author of two inspiring pro-life, pro-faith books whose central character is his second son, who was born with *spina bifida*. The books are *Waiting for Eli* and *Eli's Reach.*

He earned a Bachelor of Science degree in Secondary Education Social Studies from the University of Louisiana at Lafayette in 2001. He is married to Ashley (nee) Guillotte, and they have two small children, Ephraim and Eli. They make their home in Lafayette.

# Inspiring Books
from
# Acadian House Publishing

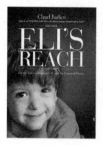

## Eli's Reach
### *On the Value of Human Life and the Power of Prayer*
*Eli's Reach* is the sequel to the inspiring heartwarming book, *Waiting for Eli*, which tells the story of a Lafayette, La., couple and their child Eli, who was born with a birth defect called *spina bifida*. It is the story of how this child's life has touched the hearts and influenced the thinking of many. Hearing Eli's story has brought about a keener appreciation of the value of all human life and is credited with saving several unborn babies from abortion.(Author: Chad Judice. ISBN: 0-925417-79-3. Price: $16.95)

## Waiting For Eli
### *A Father's Journey from Fear to Faith*
A 176-page hardcover book about a Lafayette, La., couple and their infant son Eli who was born with a dreaded birth defect called *spina bifida*. It is an inspiring story of faith, hope and the power of prayer. The book takes us on an emotional roller coaster ride, starting with the day the author first learns of his son's medical condition. This moving story has a strong pro-life, pro-love message, and is made even more compelling by the author's descriptions of little miracles along the way. (Author: Chad Judice. ISBN: 0-925417-65-3. Price: $16.95)

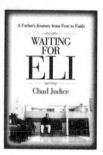

## Dying In God's Hands
A 152-page hardcover book that provides keen insights into the hearts and minds of the dying. It is based on a dozen or more interviews with terminally ill hospice patients, in which they share their hopes, dreams, fears and needs. The majority of the interviews provide evidence that faith in God and belief in the hereafter are the greatest strengths of the dying. Designed to comfort the dying and their loved ones, the book also contains a section of prayers and prose from all major world religions. (Author: Camille Pavy Claibourne. ISBN: 0-925417-64-5. Price: $16.95)

## Freedom From Fear
### *A Way Through The Ways of Jesus The Christ*

Everyone at one time or another feels fear, guilt, worry and shame. But when these emotions get out of control they can enslave a person, literally taking over his or her life. In this 142-page softcover book, the author suggests that the way out of this bondage is prayer, meditation and faith in God and His promise of salvation. The author points to the parables in the Gospels as Jesus' antidote to fears of various kinds, citing the parables of the prodigal son, the good Samaritan, and the widow and the judge. Exercises at the end of each chapter help make the book's lessons all the more real and useful. (Author: Francis Vanderwall. ISBN: 0-925417-34-3. Price: $14.95)

## Grand Coteau
### *The Holy Land of South Louisiana*

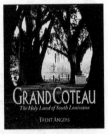

A 176-page hardcover book that captures the spirit of one of the truly holy places in North America. It is a town of mystery, with well-established ties to the supernatural, including the famous Miracle of Grand Coteau. Brought to life by dozens of exceptional color photographs, the book focuses on the town's major religious institutions: The Academy of the Sacred Heart, Our Lady of the Oaks Retreat House and St. Charles College/Jesuit Spirituality Center. The book explores not only the history of these three institutions but also the substance of their teachings. (Author: Trent Angers. ISBN: 0-925417-47-5. Price: $44.95)

## Getting Over the 4 Hurdles of Life

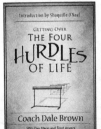

A 160-page hardcover book that shows us ways to get past the obstacles, or hurdles, that block our path to success, happiness and peace of mind. Four of the most common hurdles are "I can't / You can't," past failures or fear of failure, handicaps, and lack of self-knowledge. This inspiring book – by one of the top motivational speakers in the U.S. – is brought to life by intriguing stories of various people who overcame life's hurdles. Introduction by former LSU and NBA star Shaquille O'Neal. (Author: Coach Dale Brown. ISBN: 0-925417-72-6. Price: $17.95)

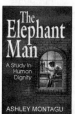